Vunzi

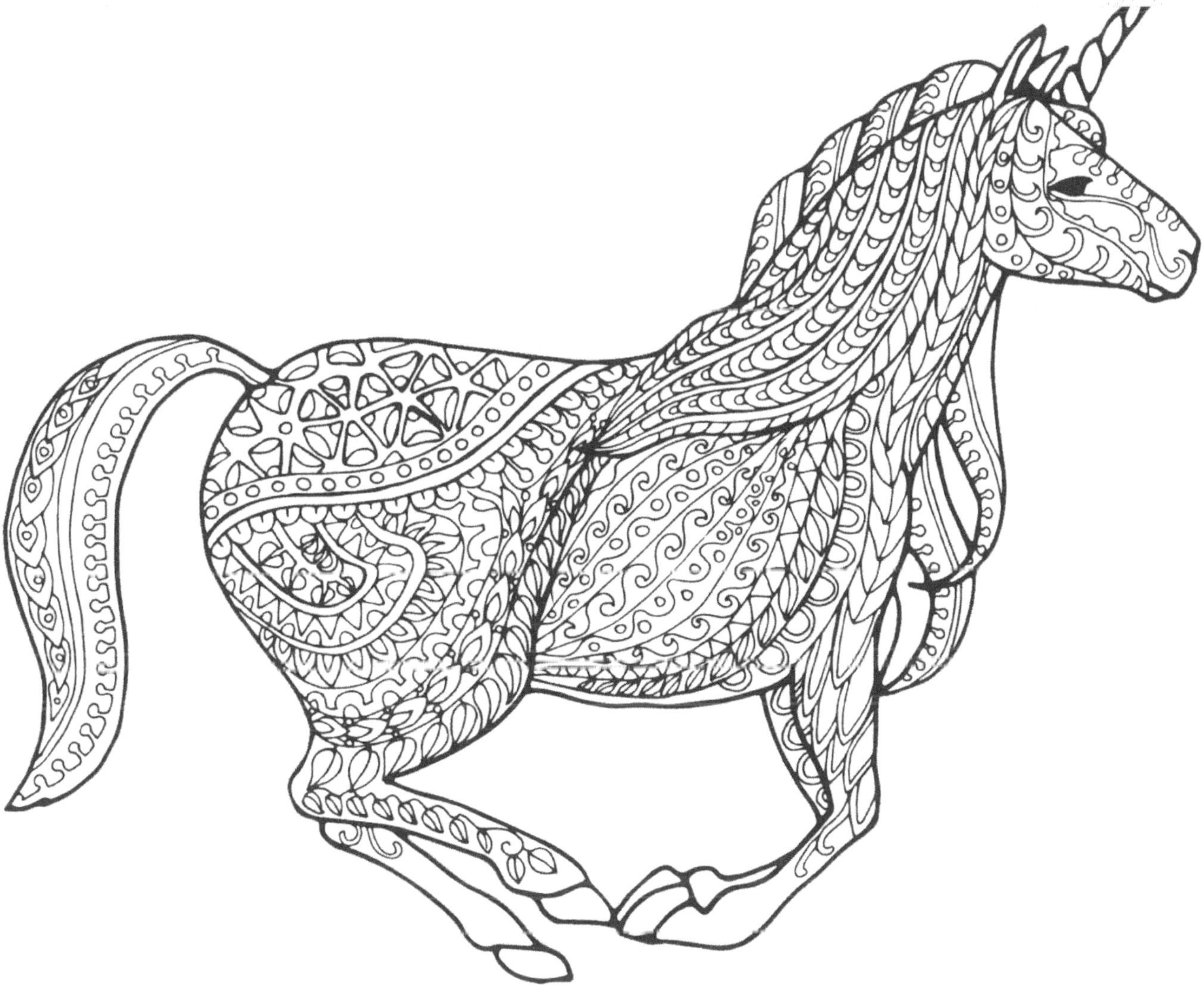

UNICORN

Coloring Book For Adults

ISBN-13: 978-1-0723-6360-6

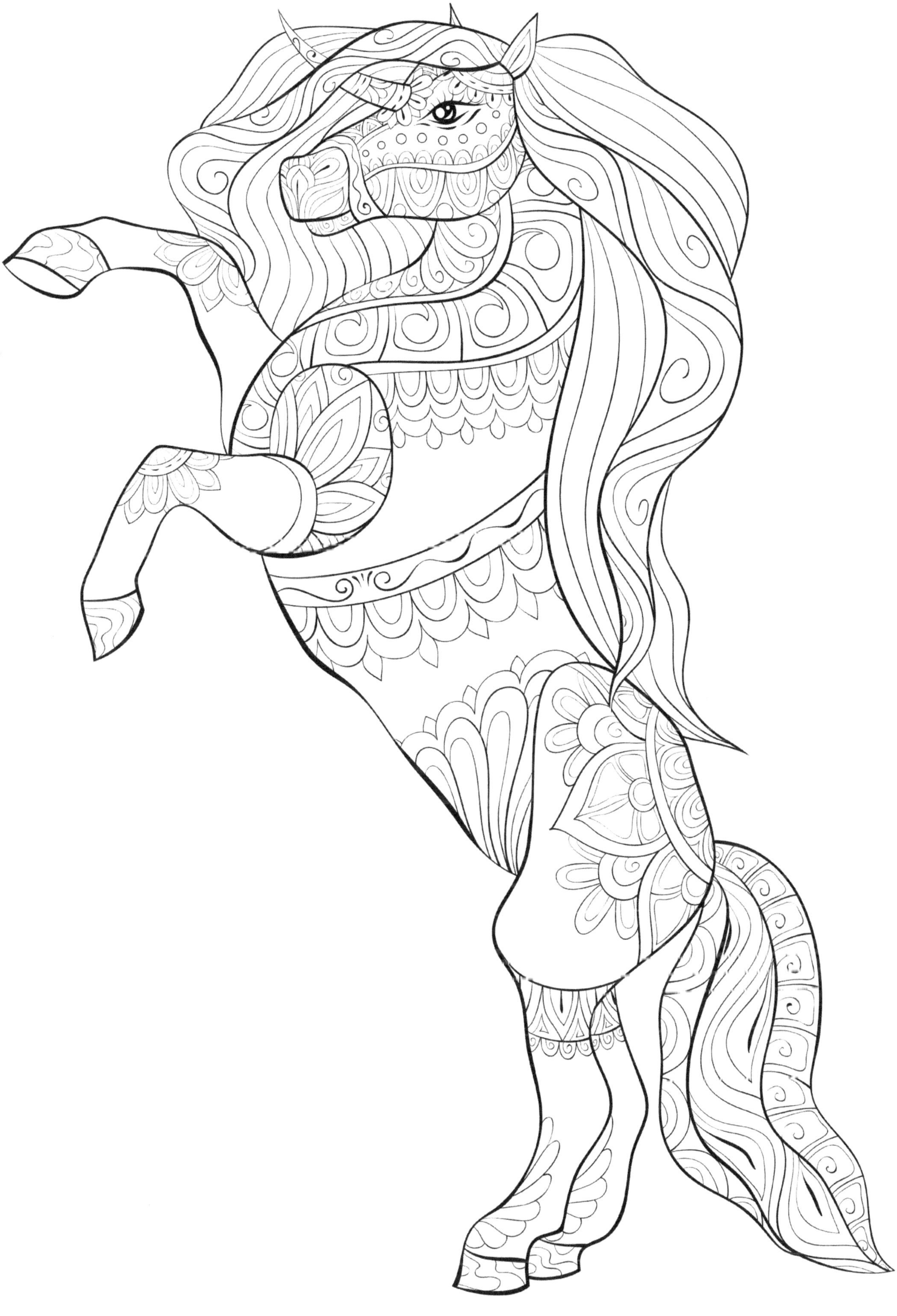

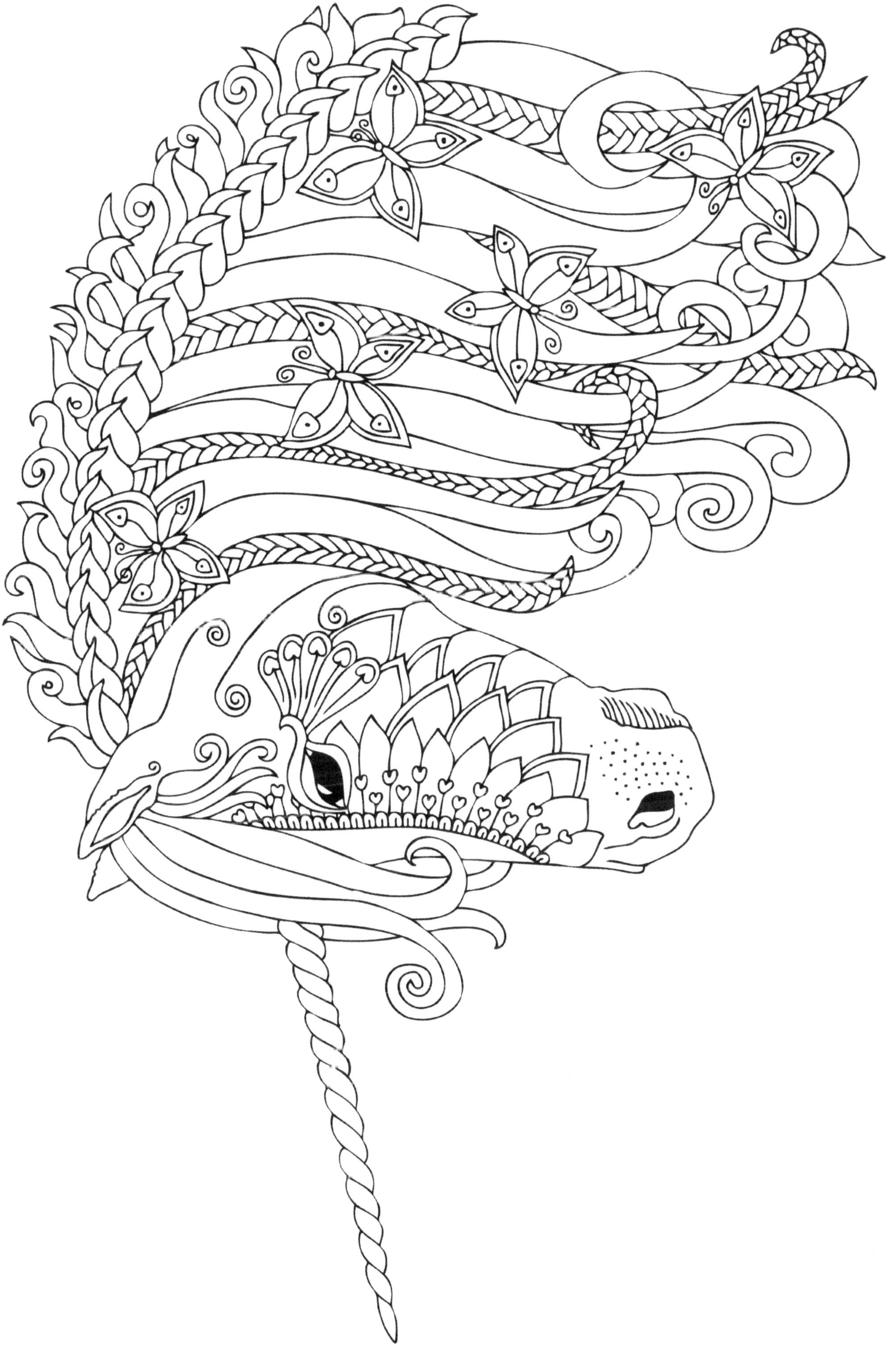

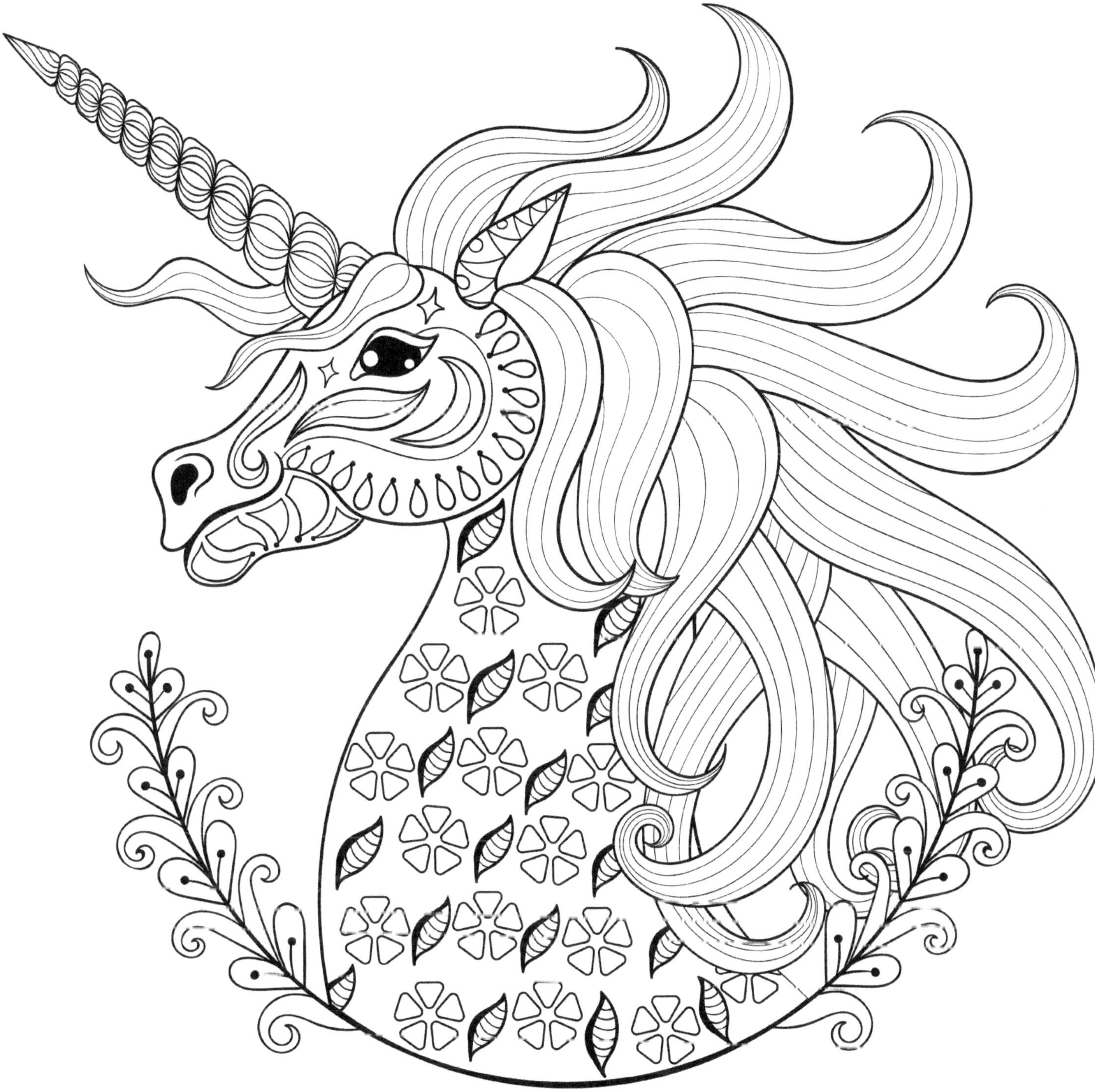

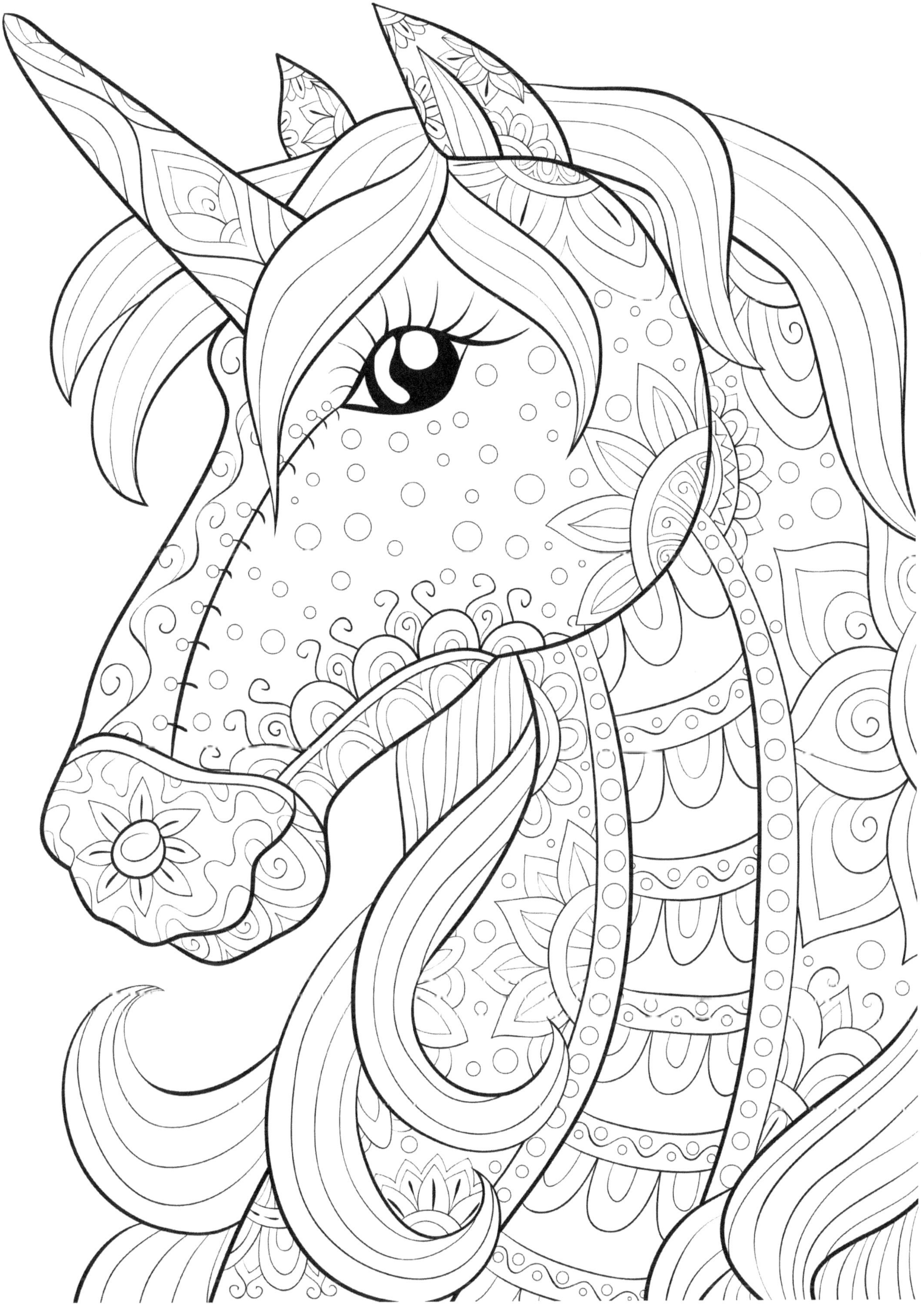

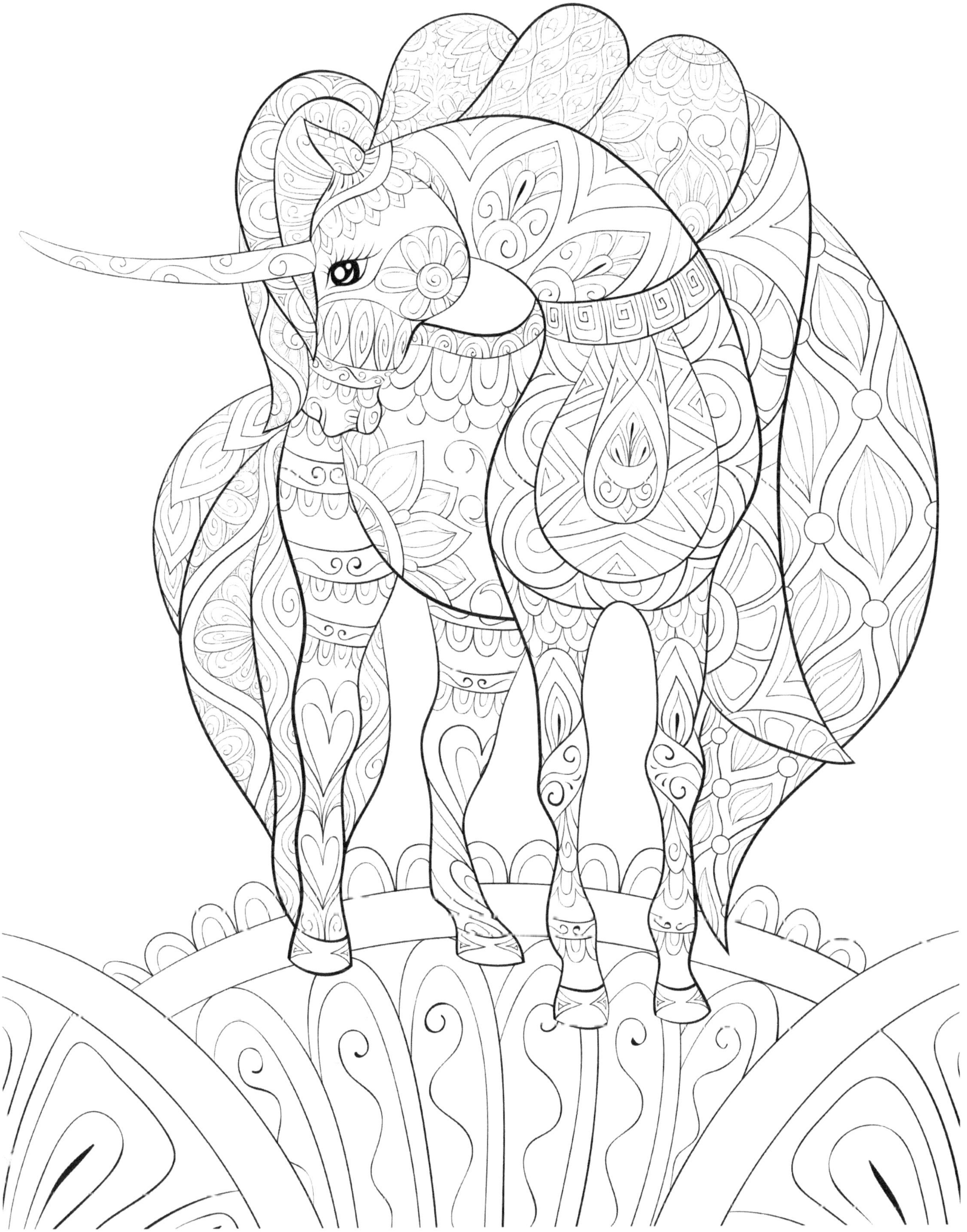

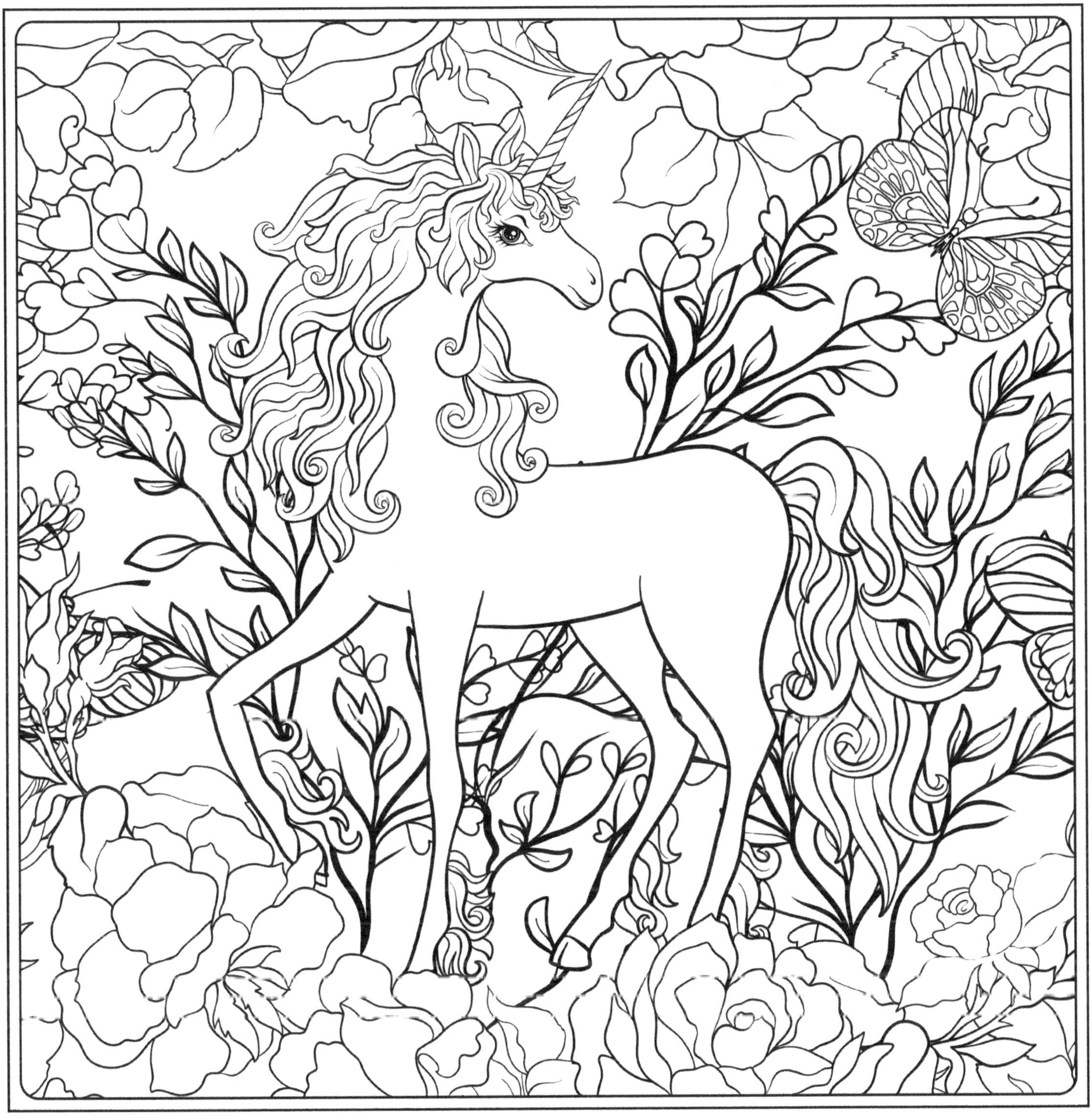

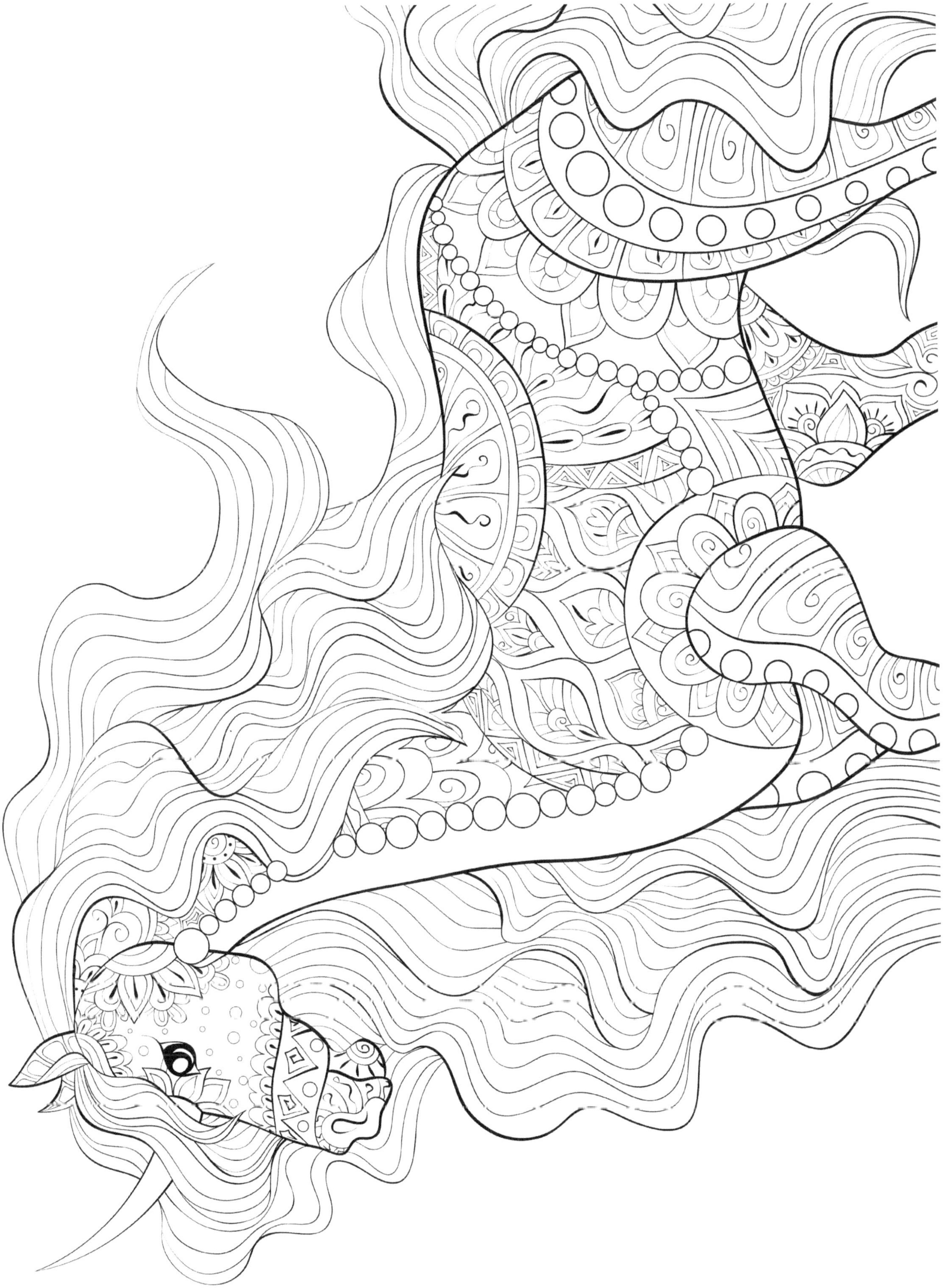

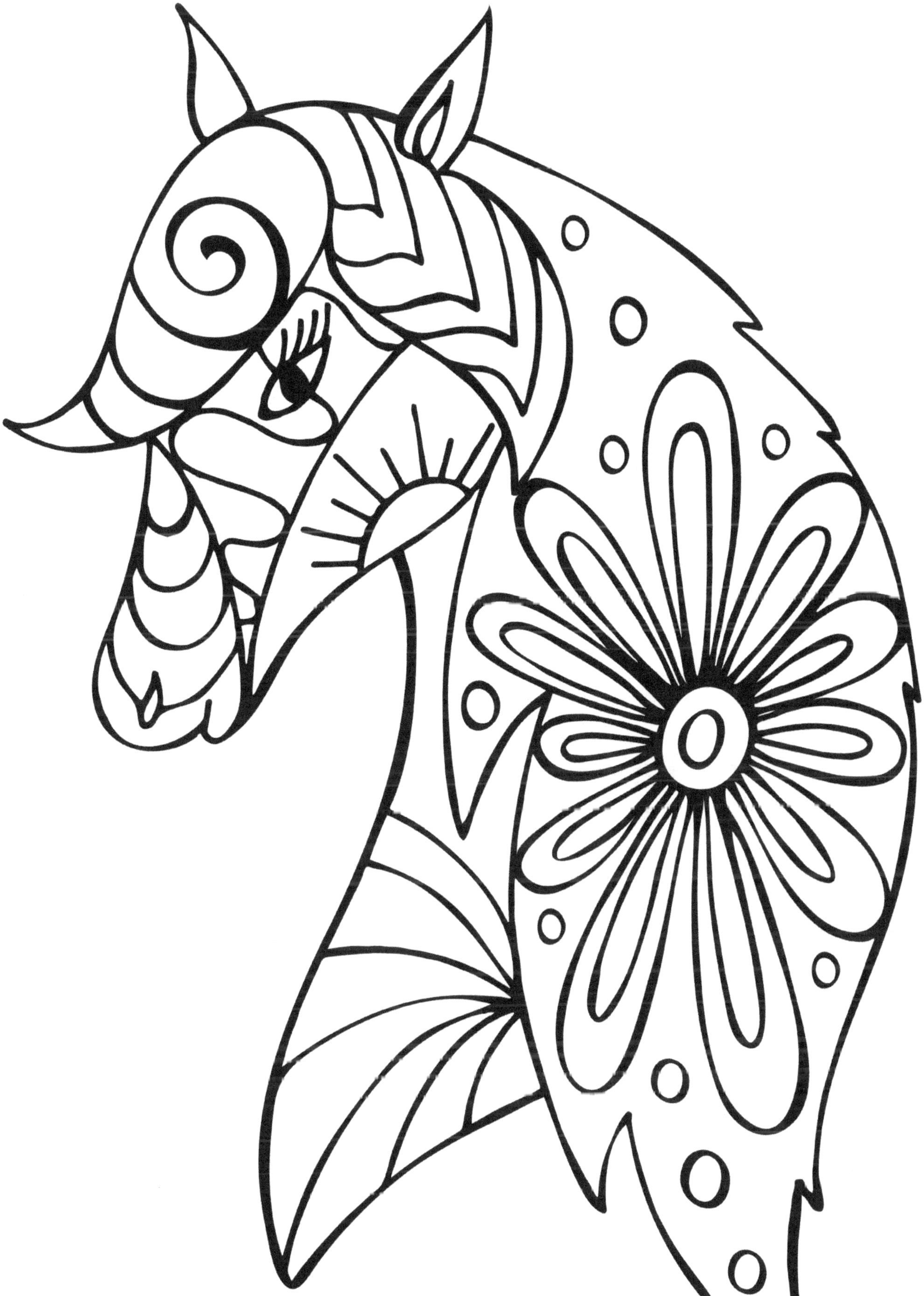

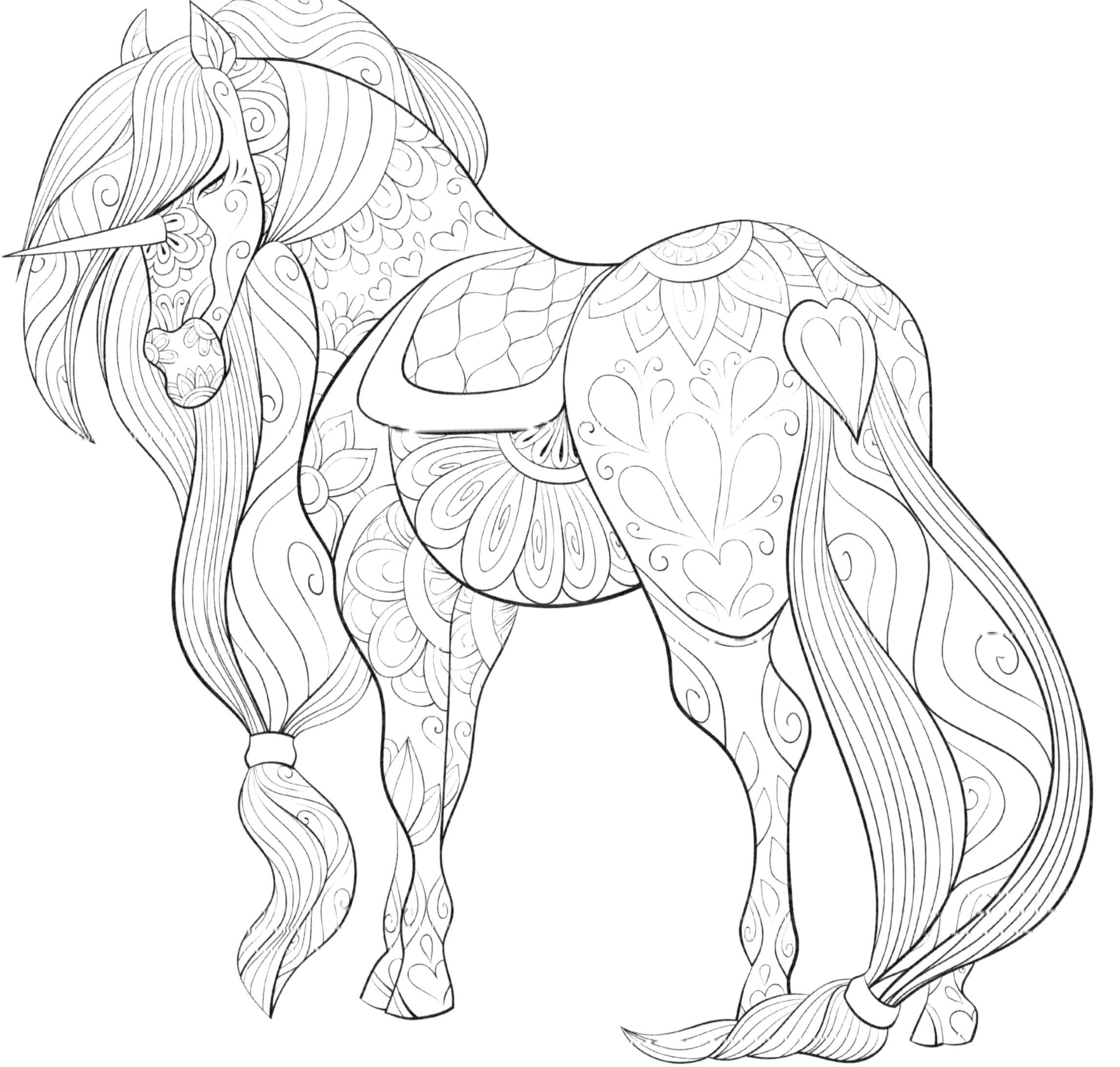

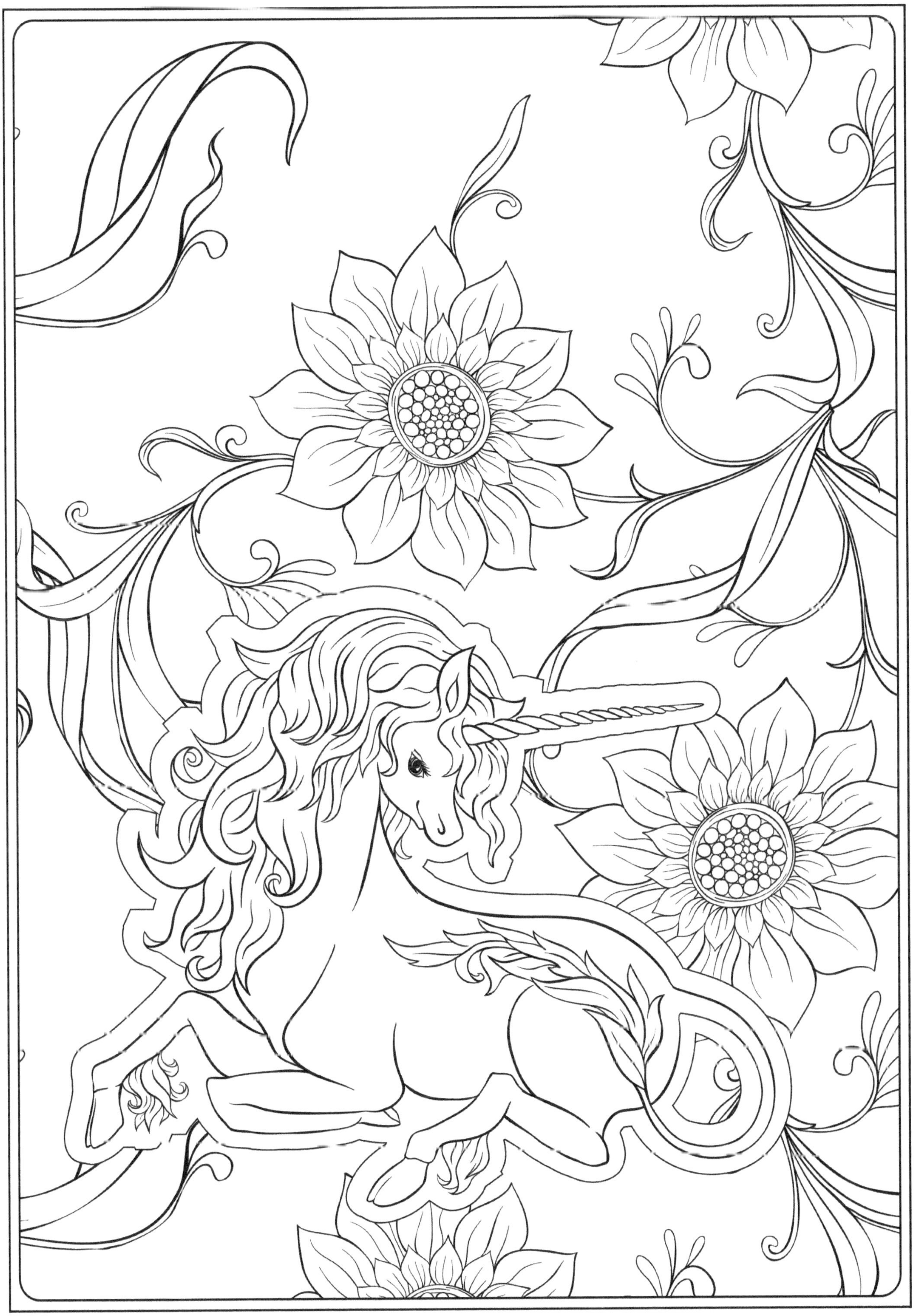

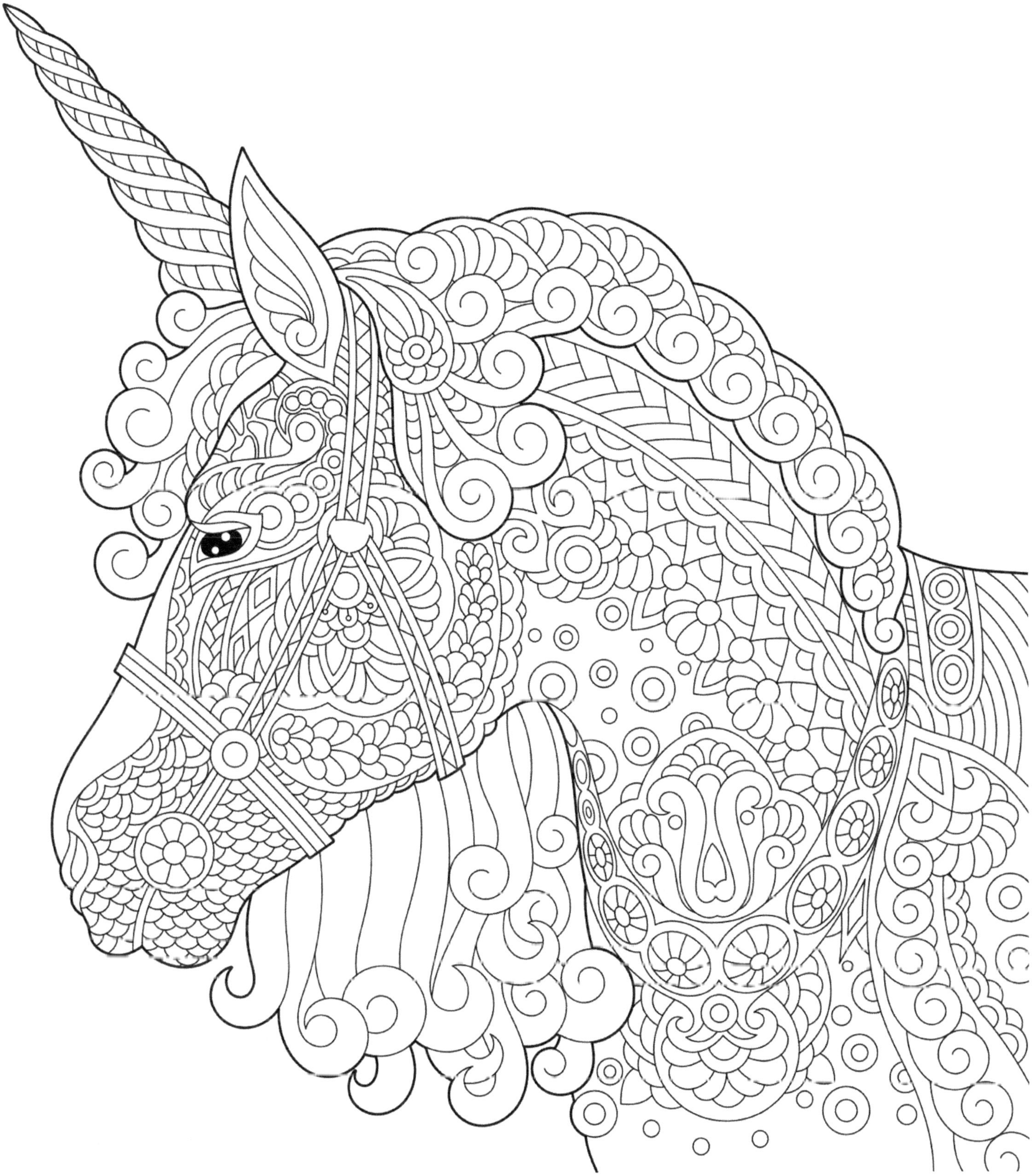

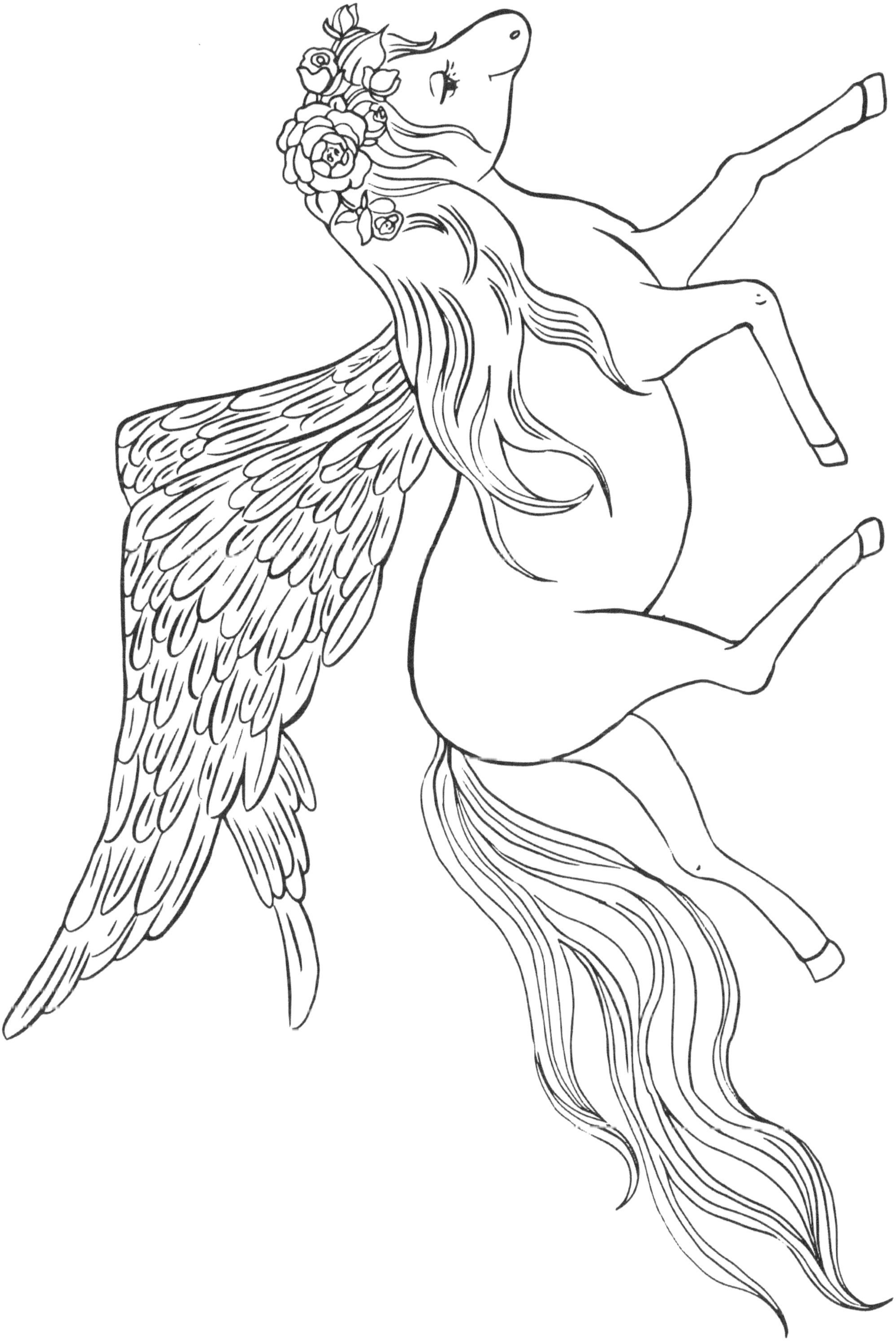

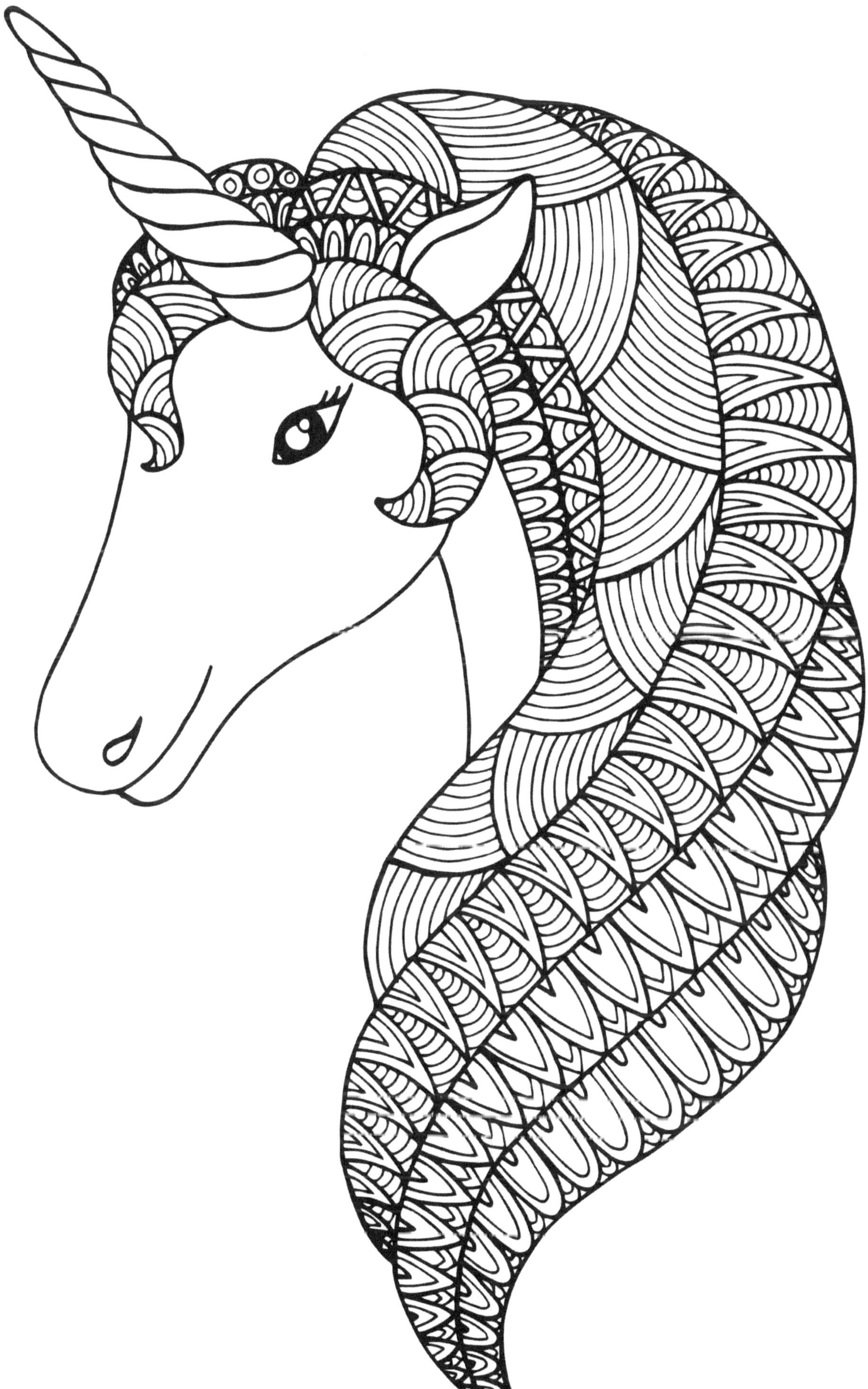

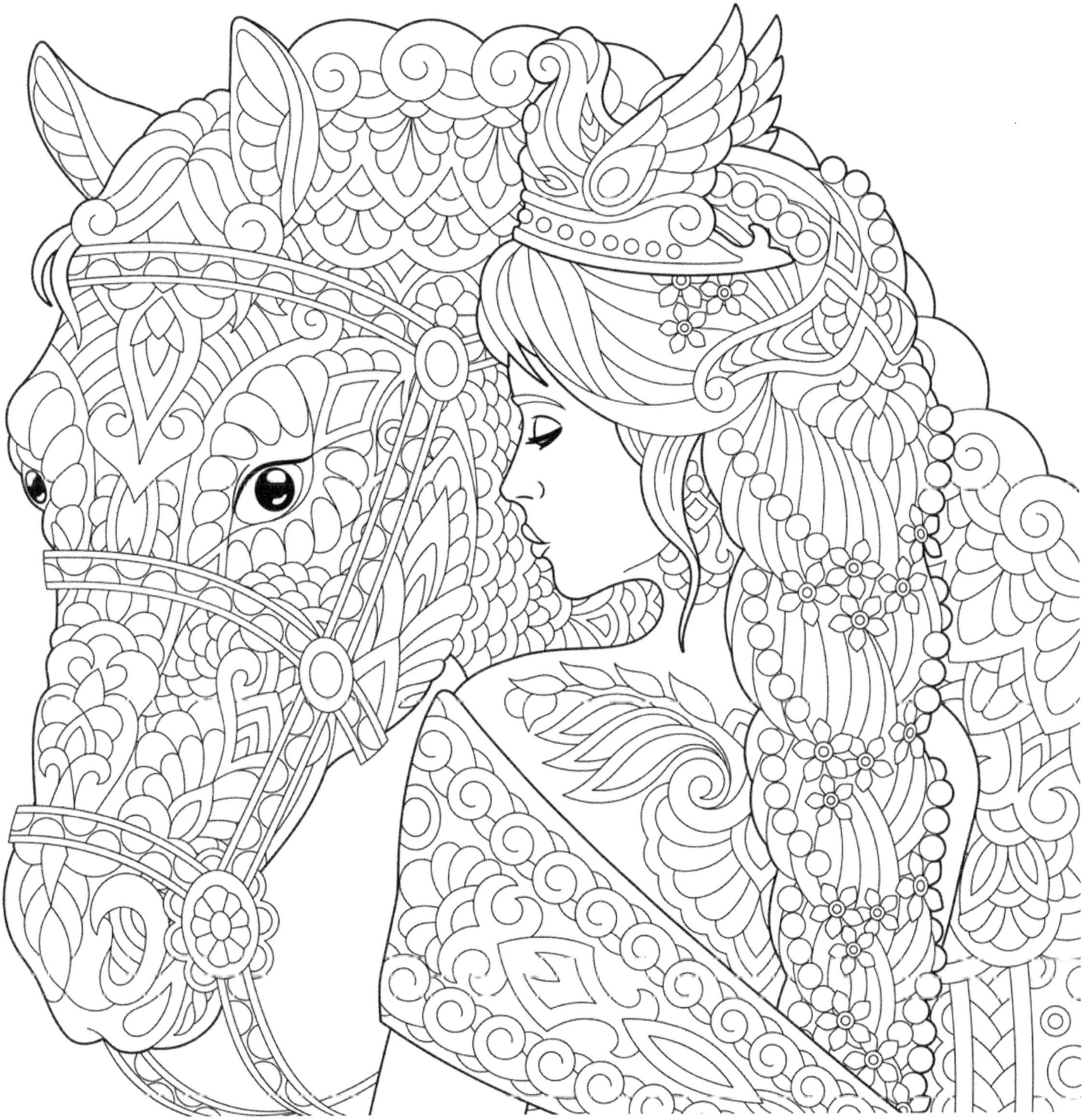

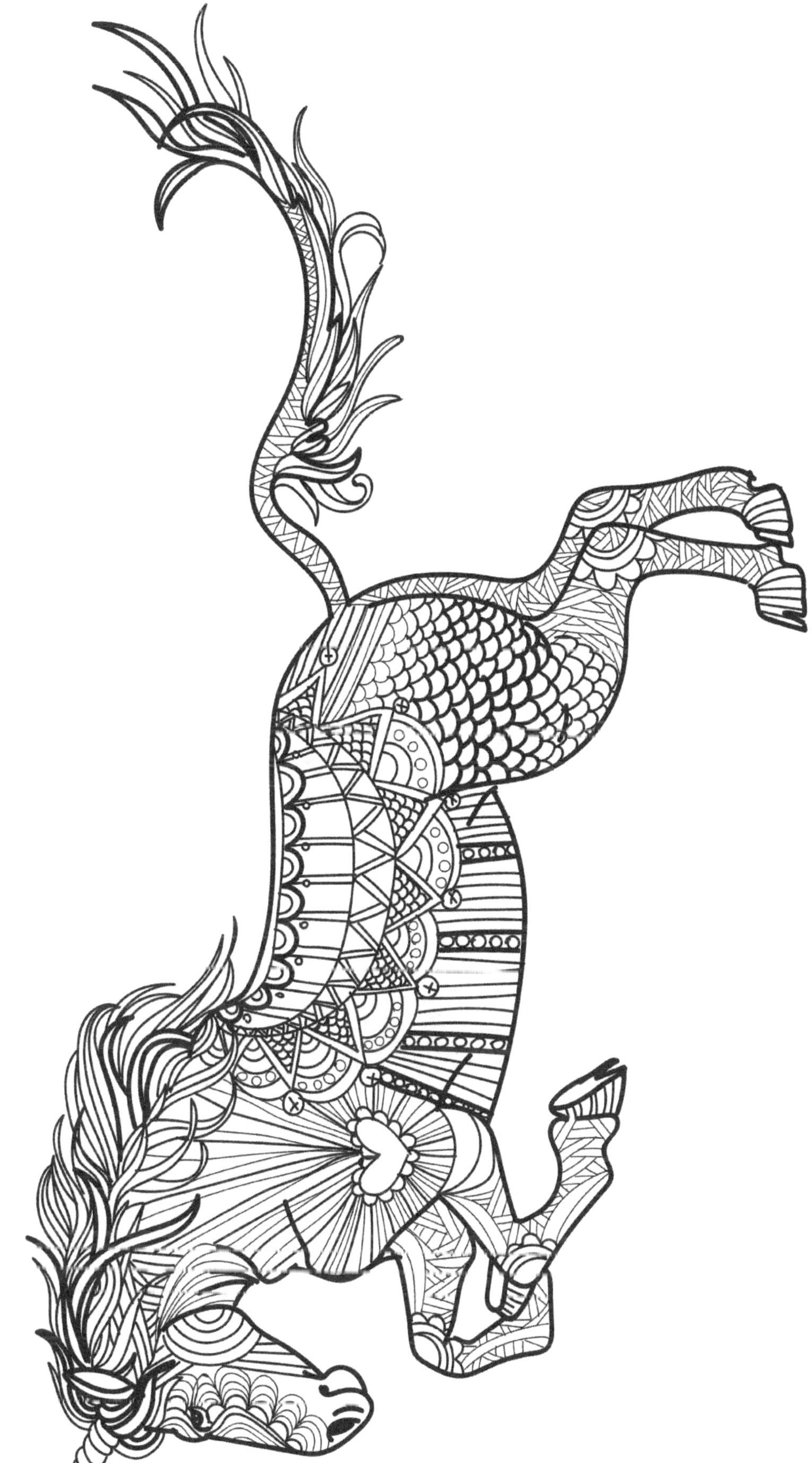

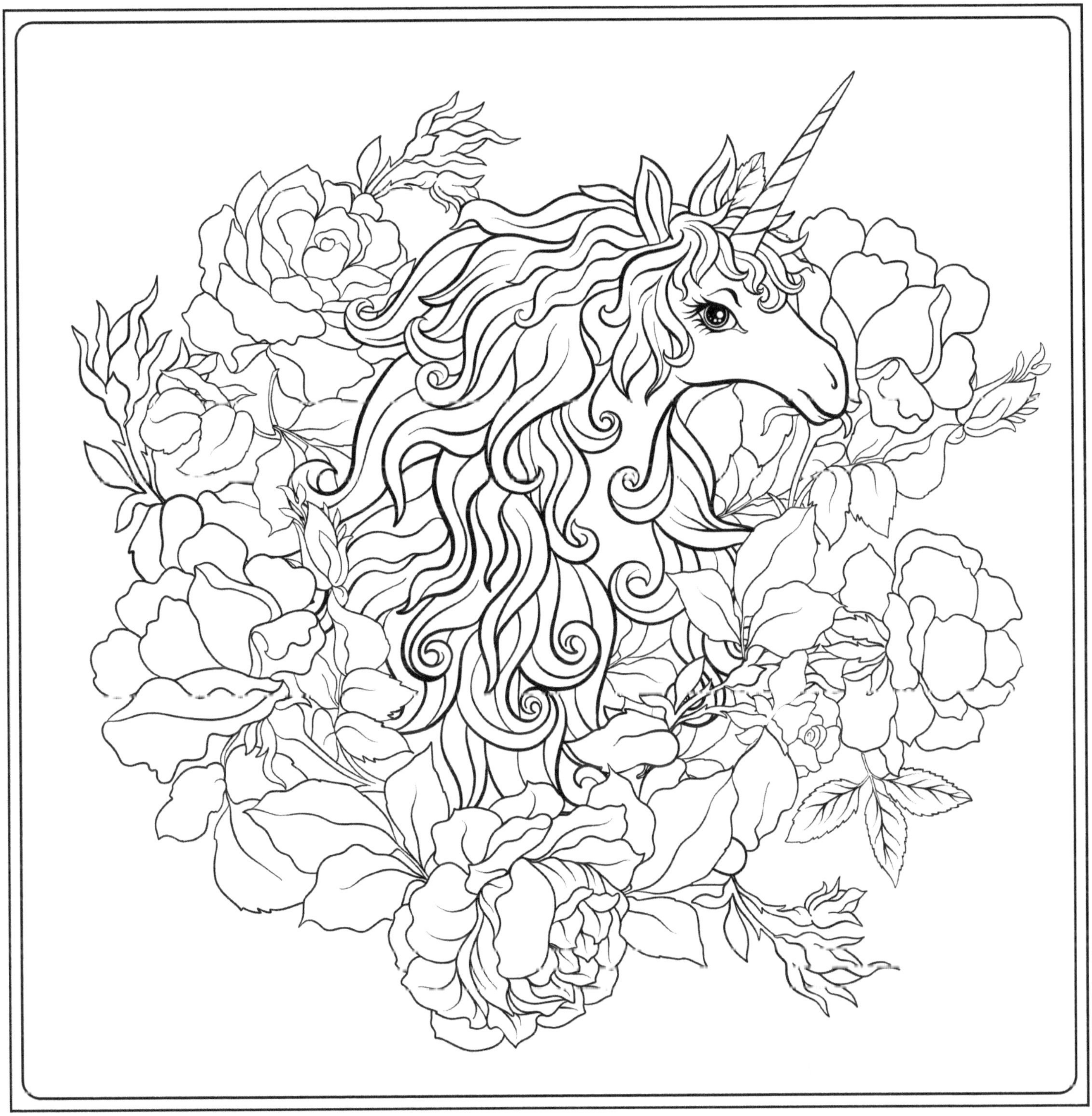

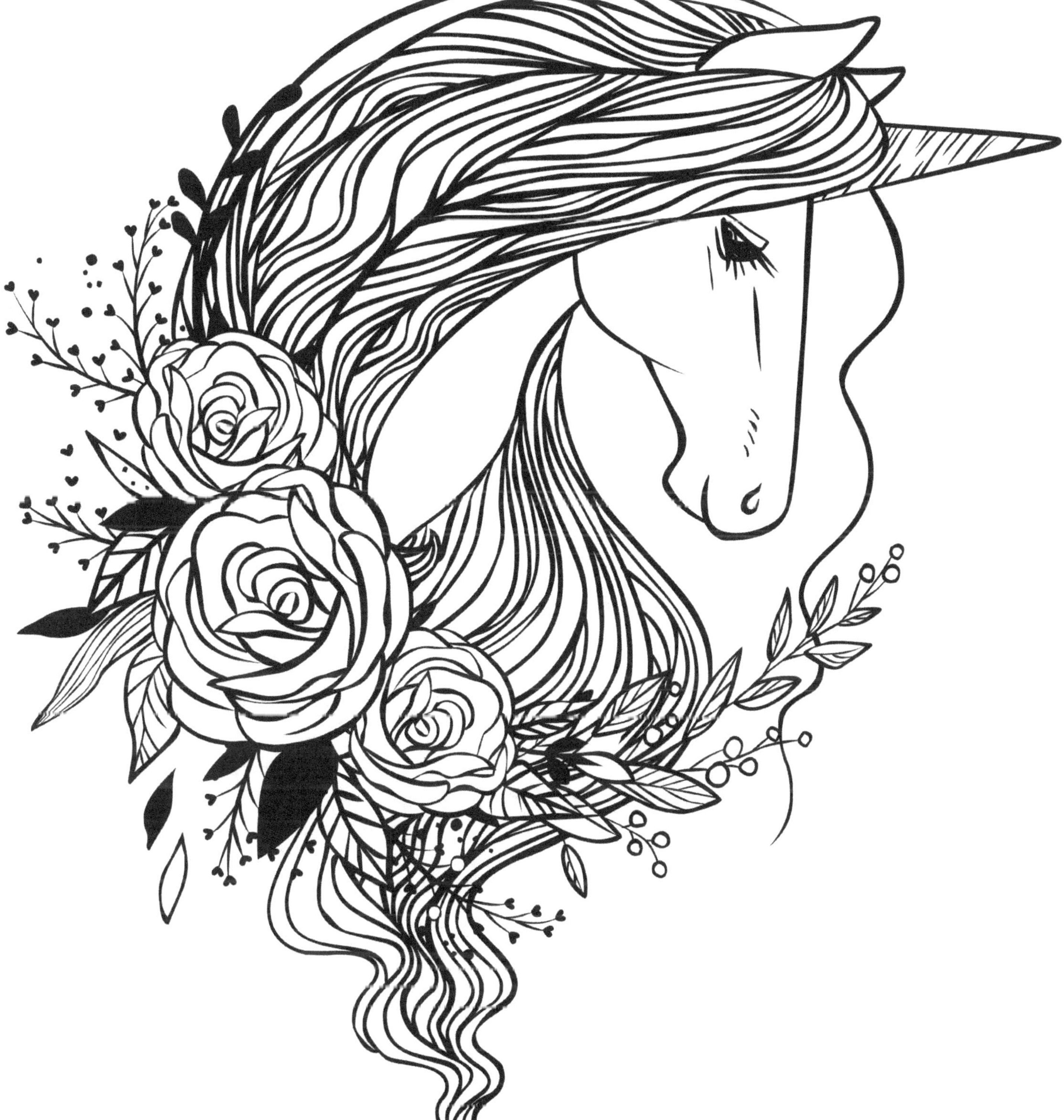

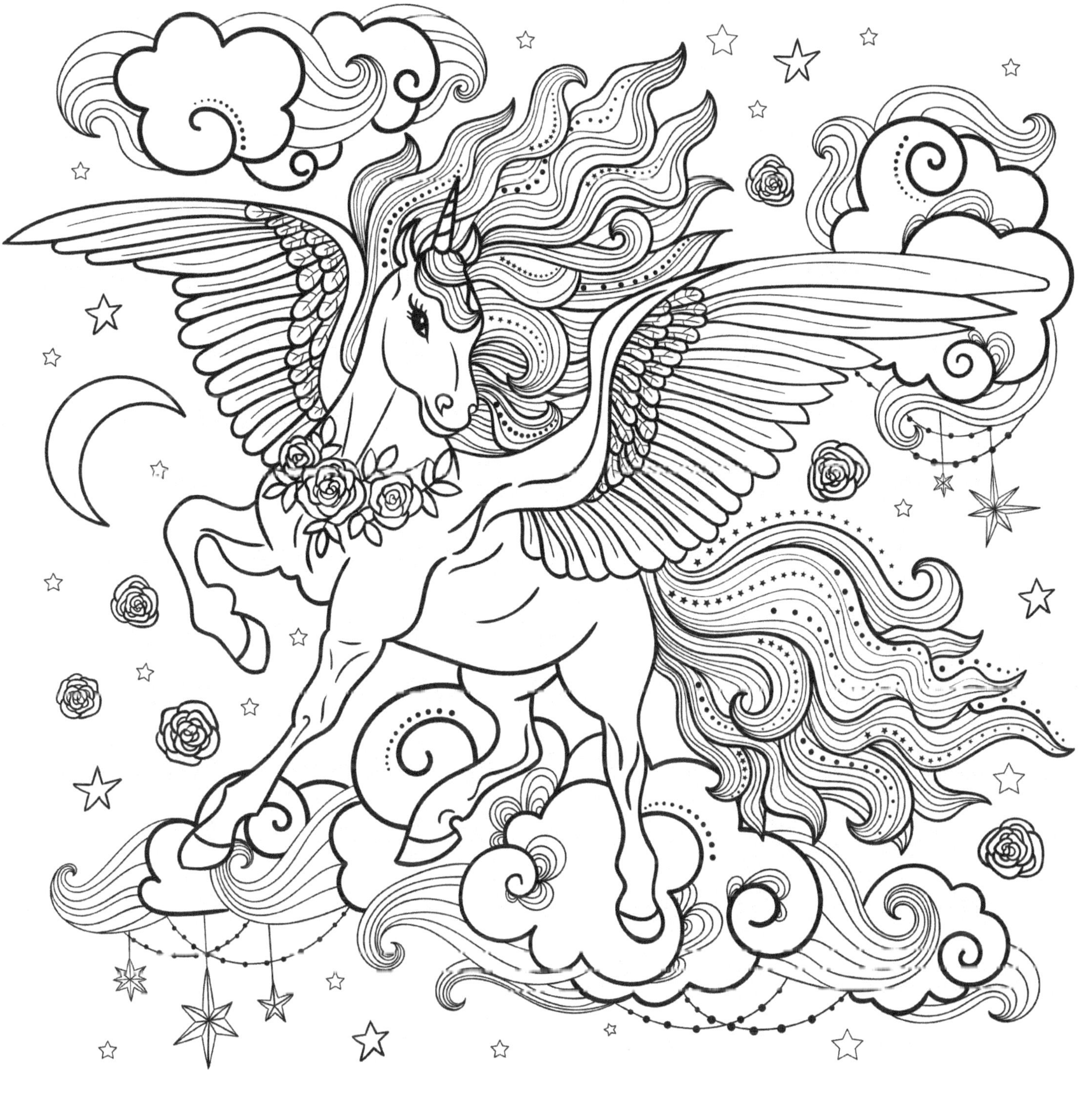

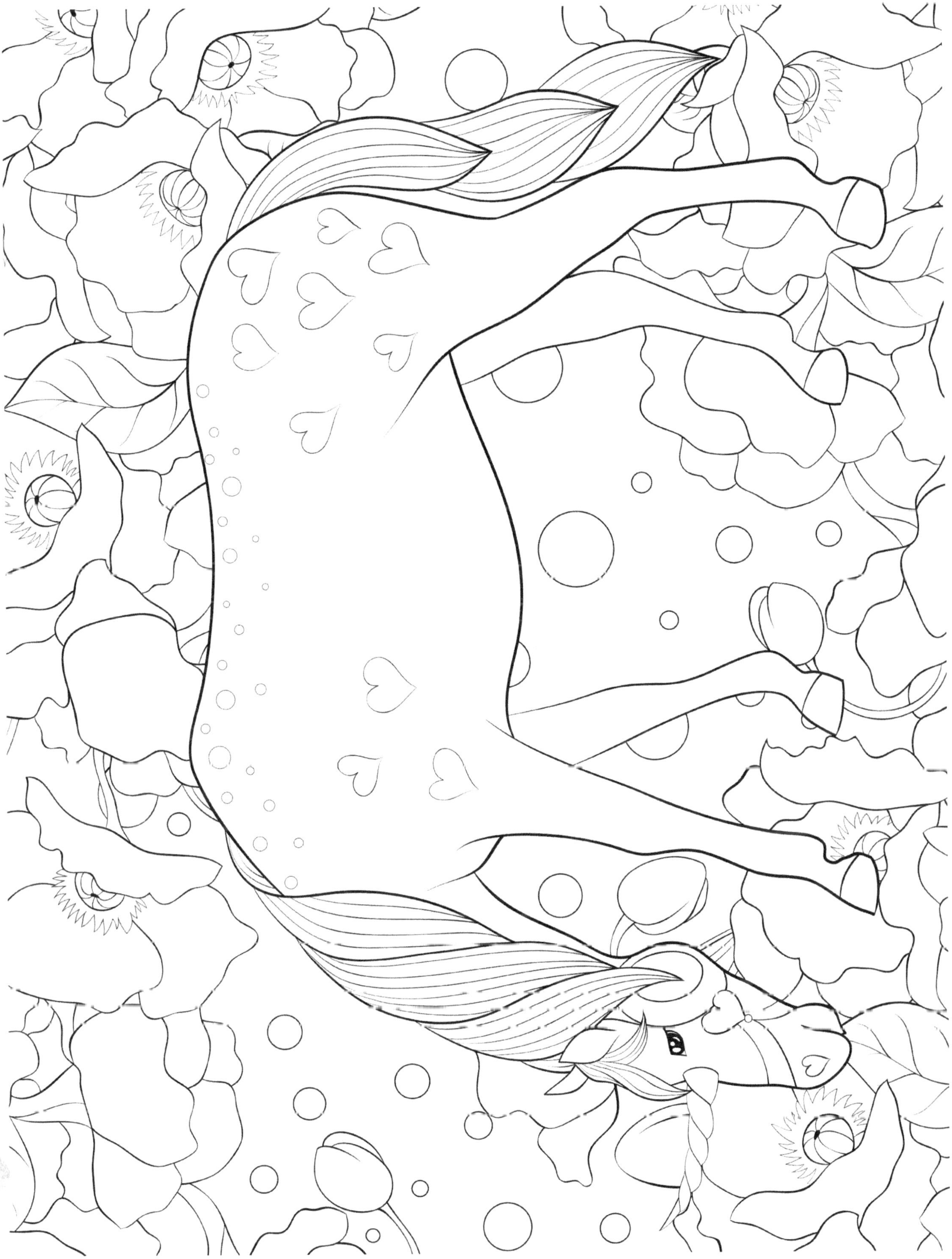

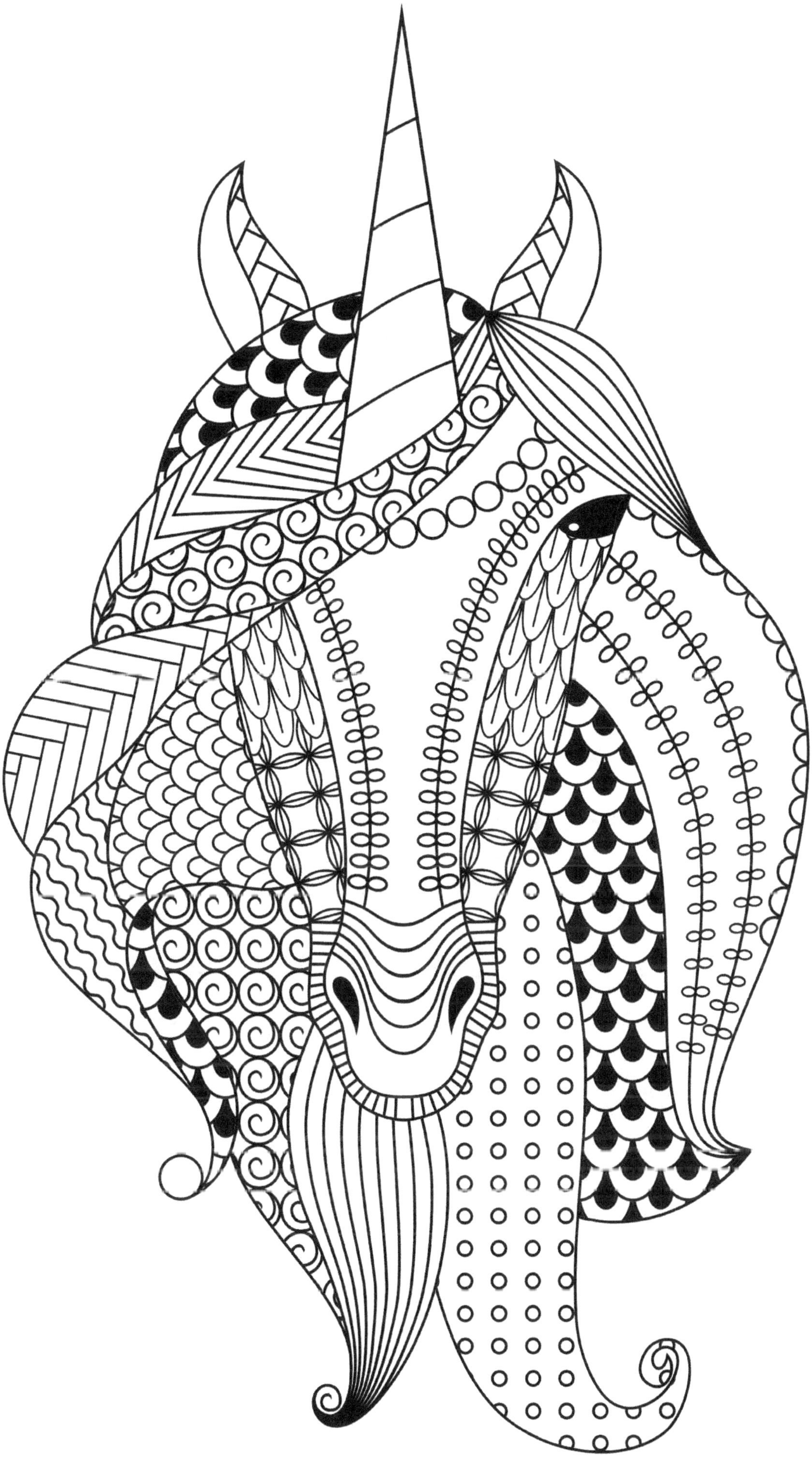

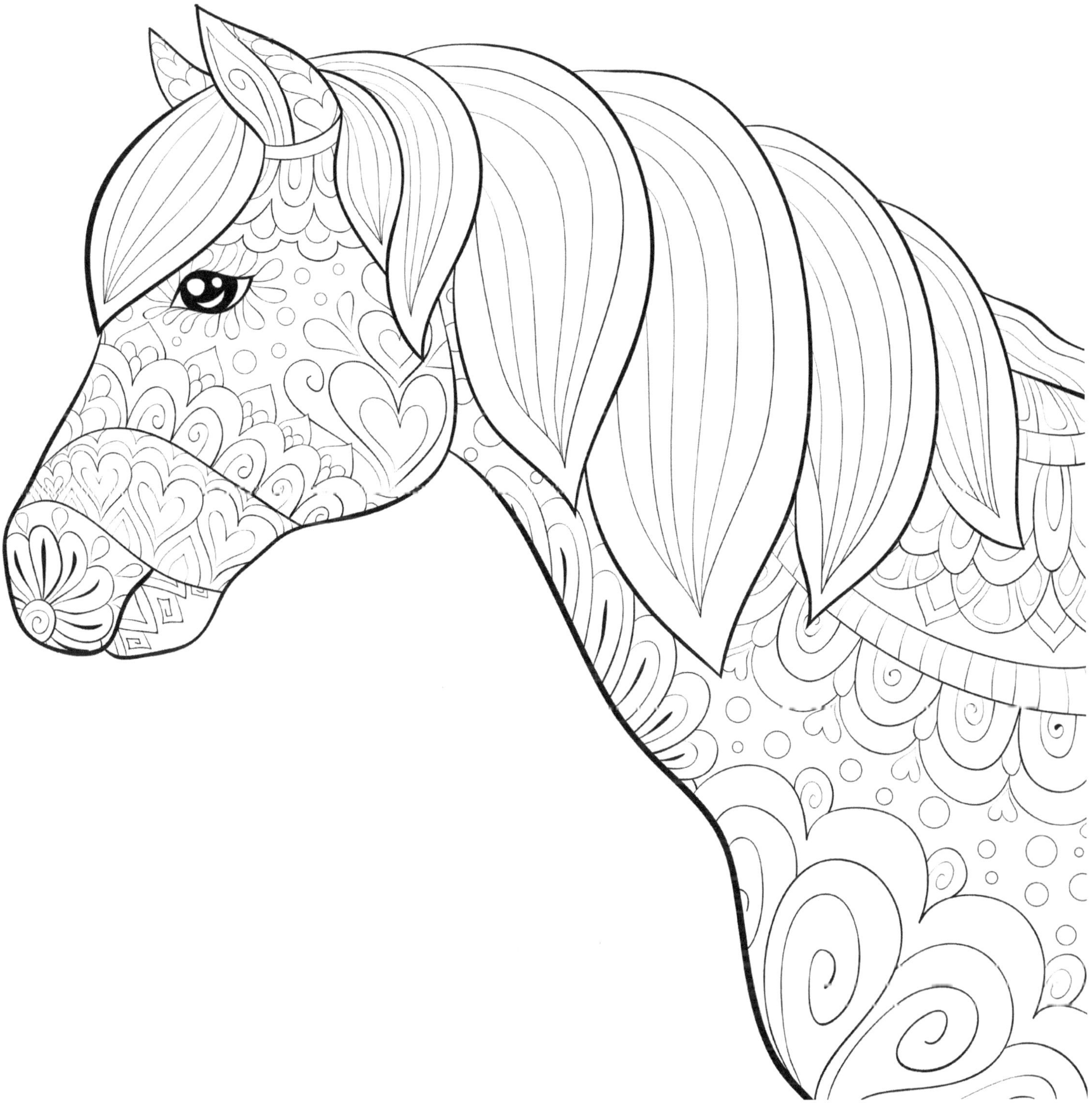

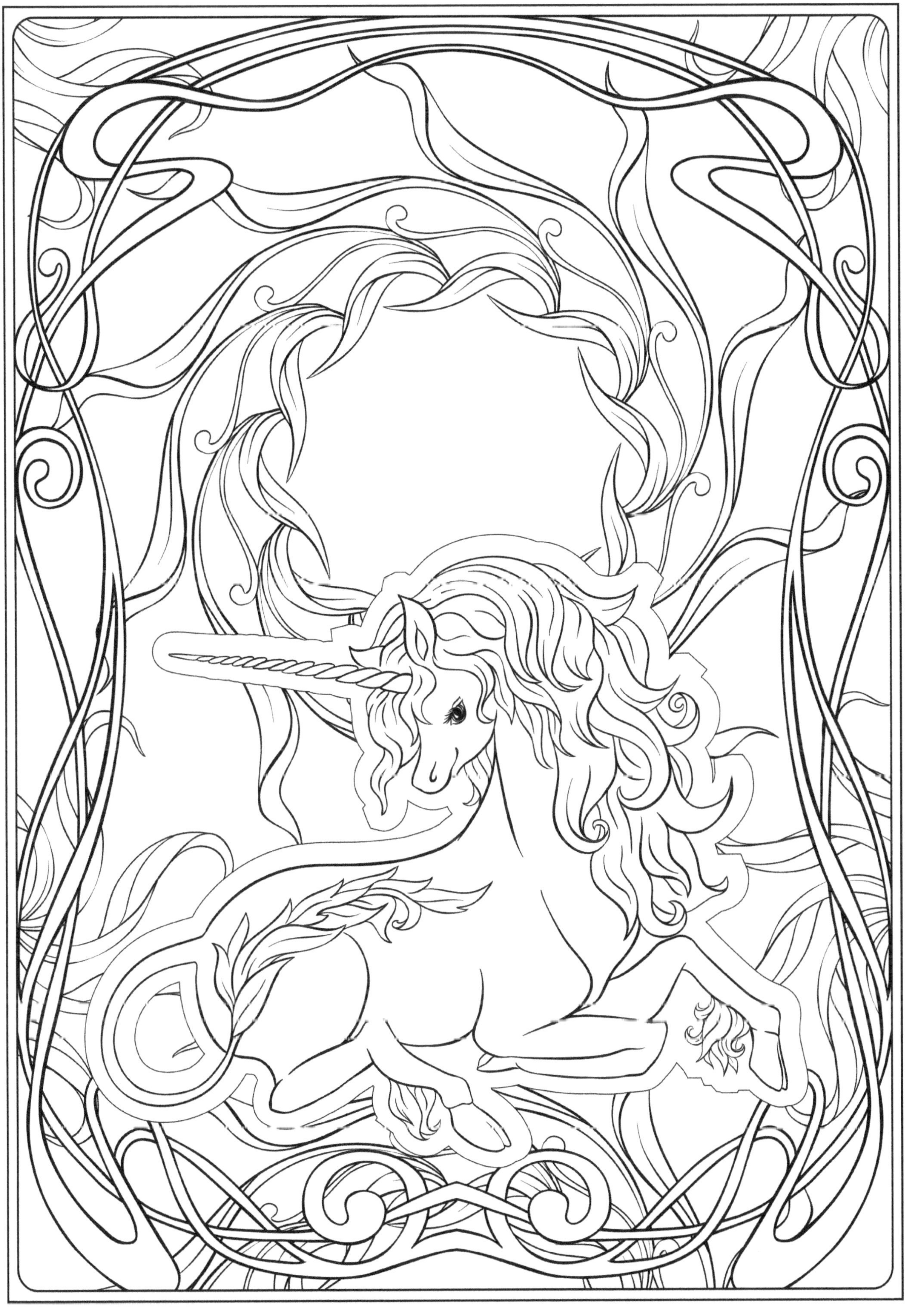

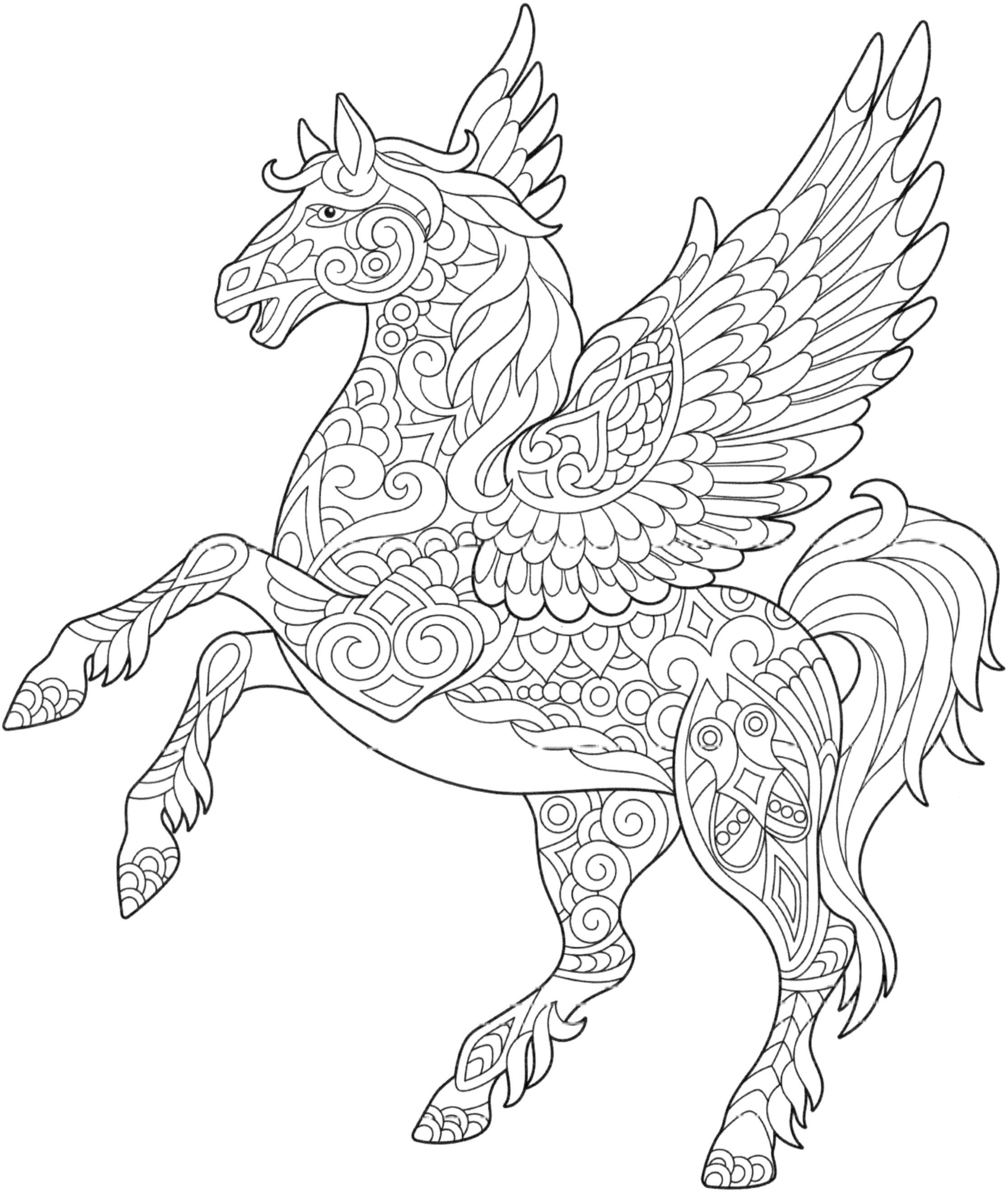

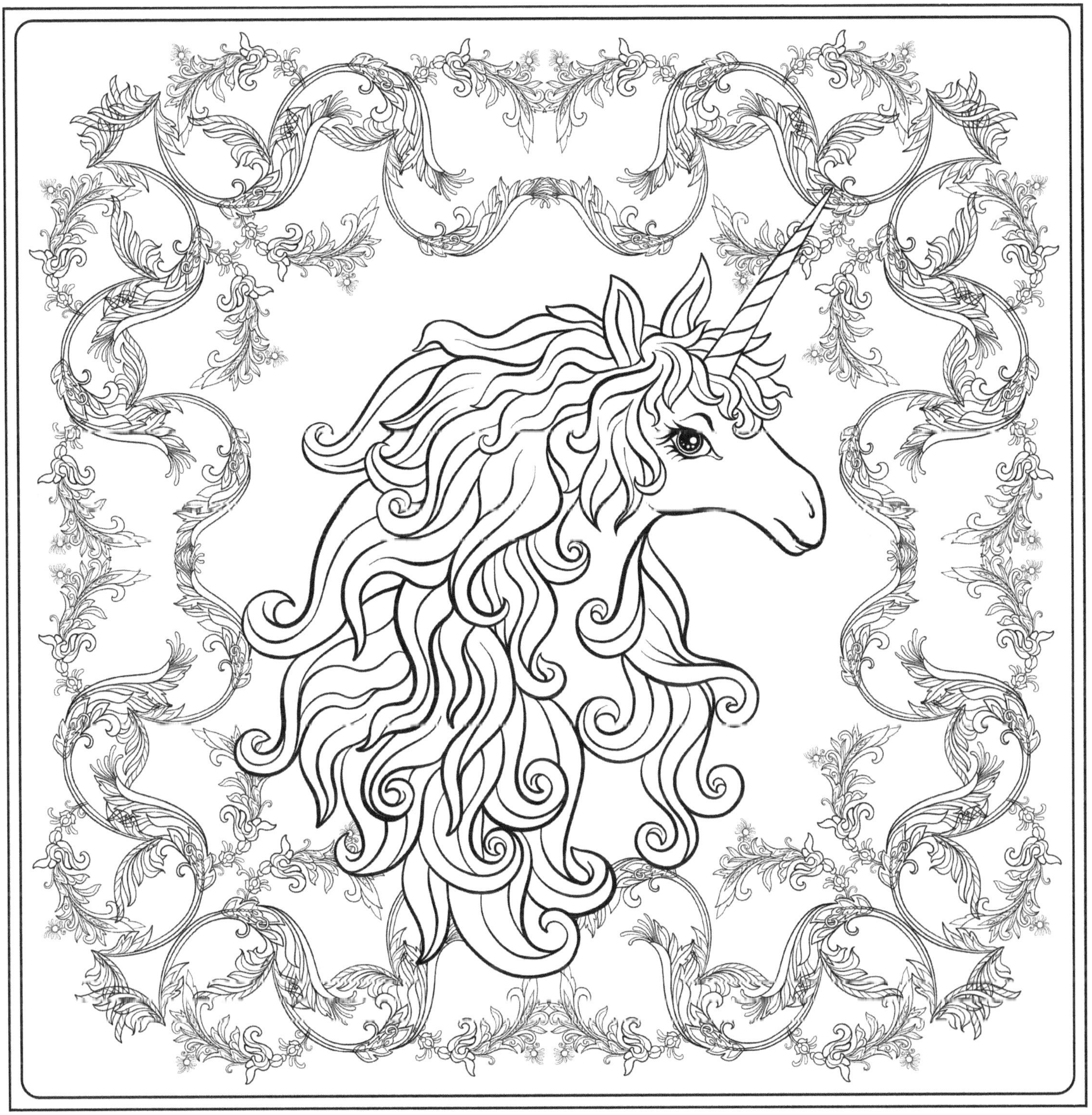

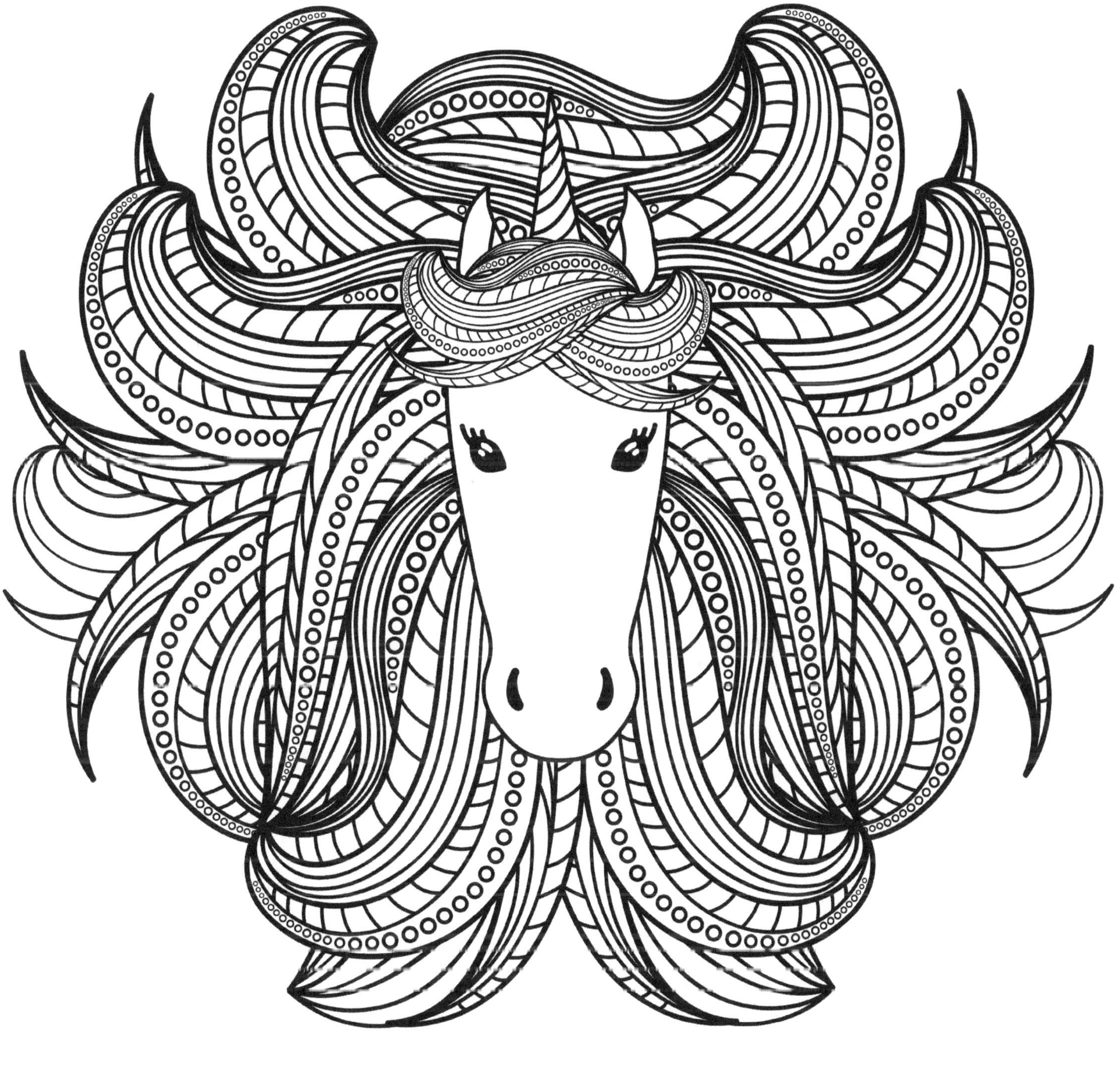

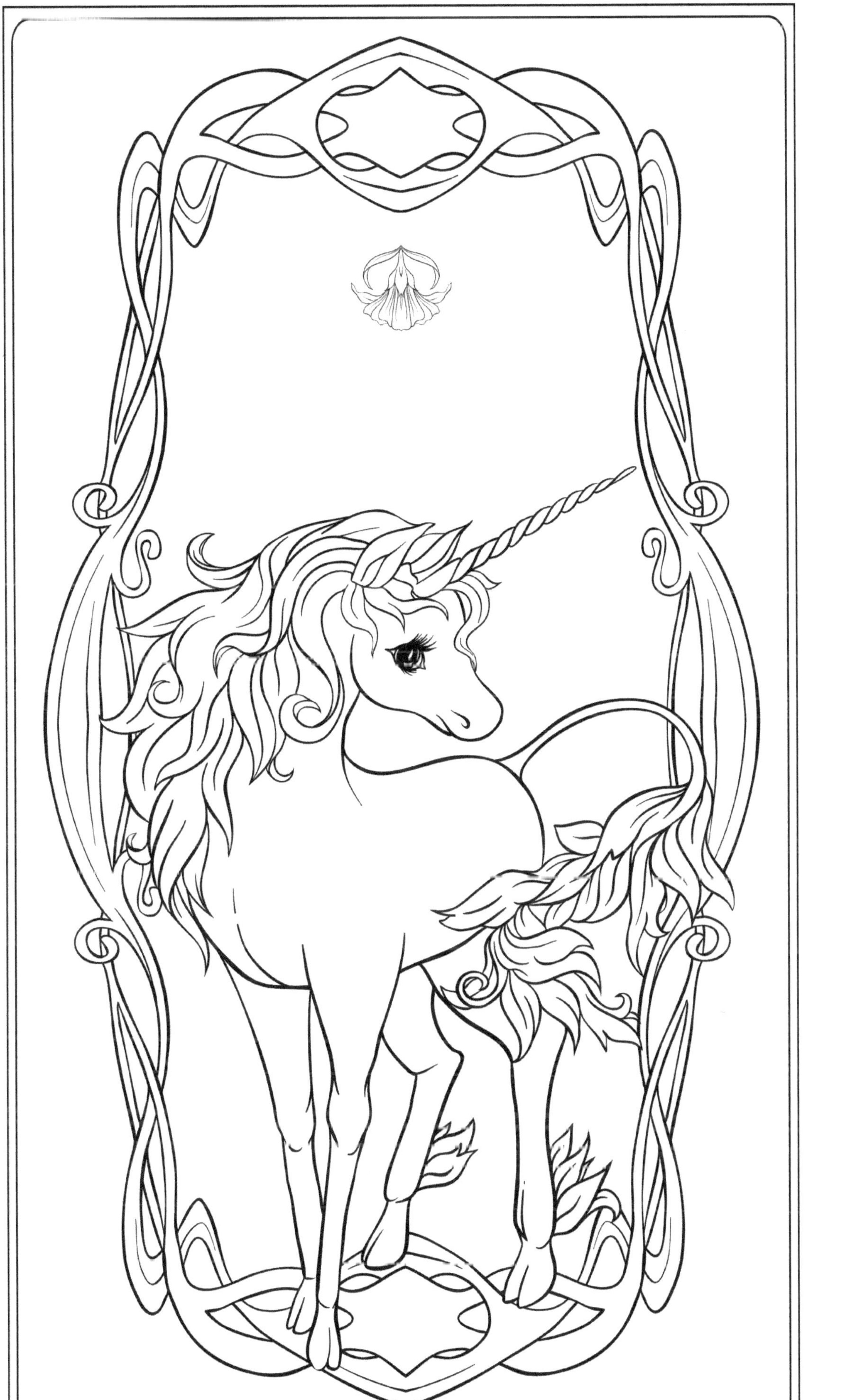

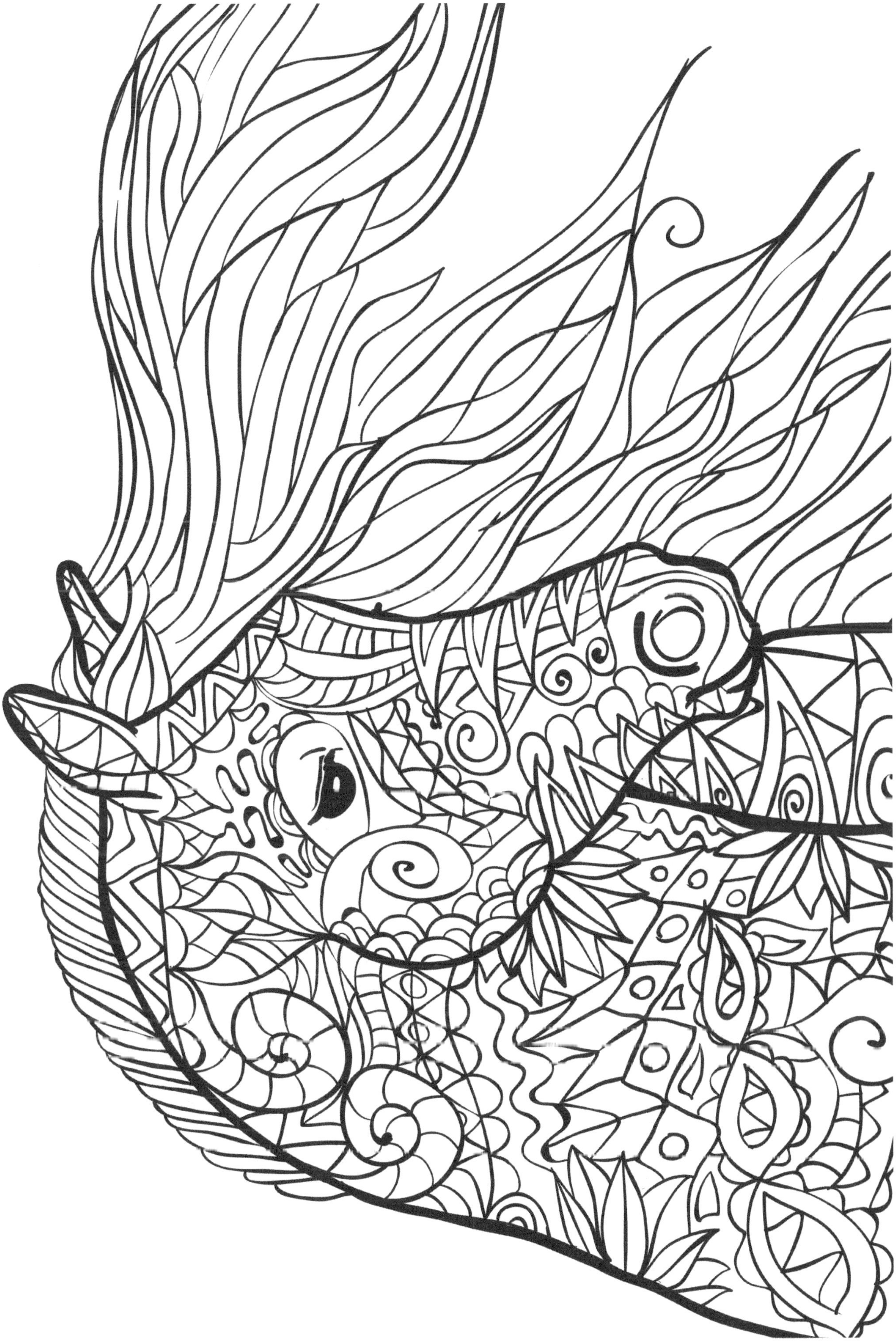

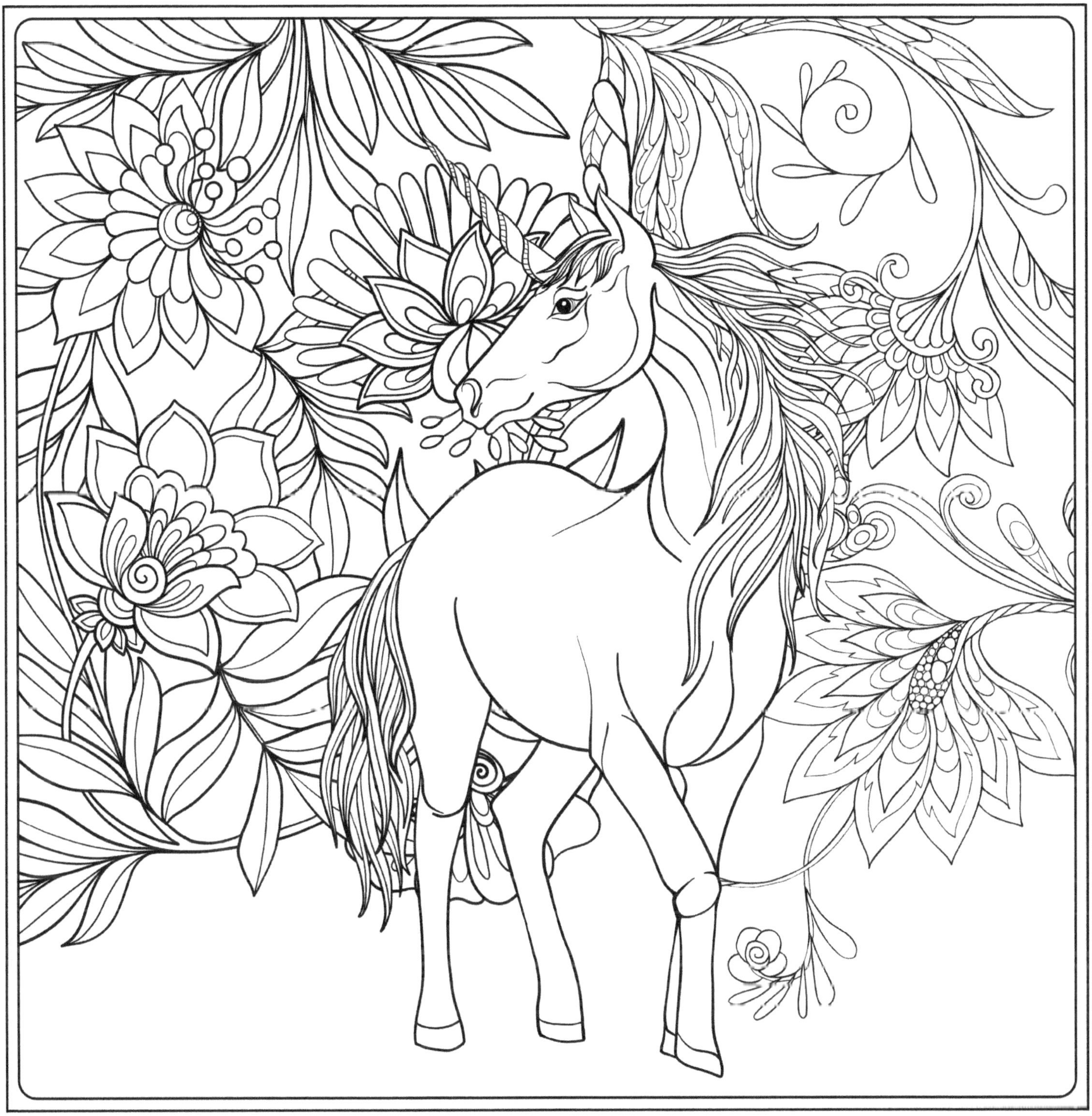

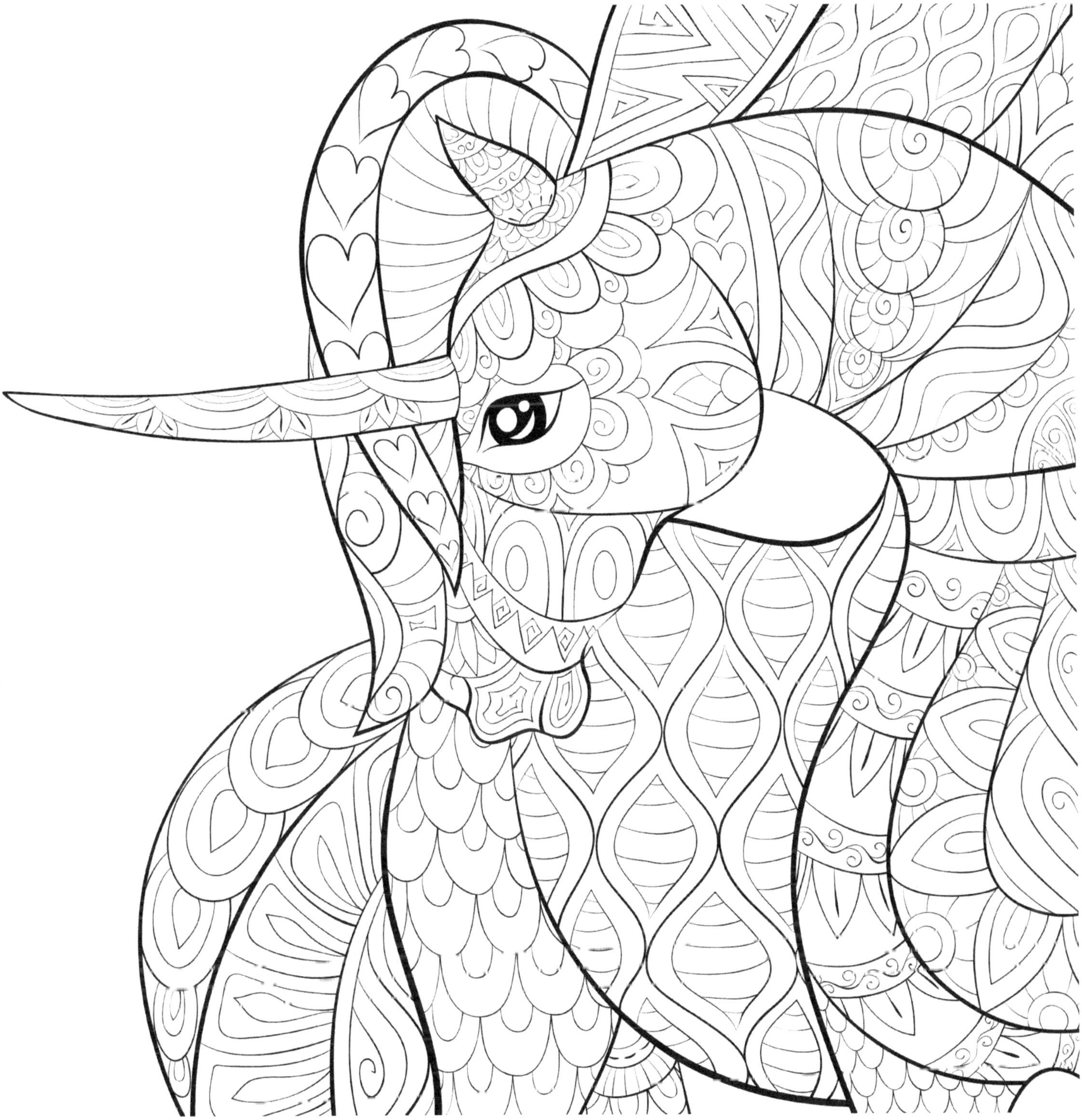

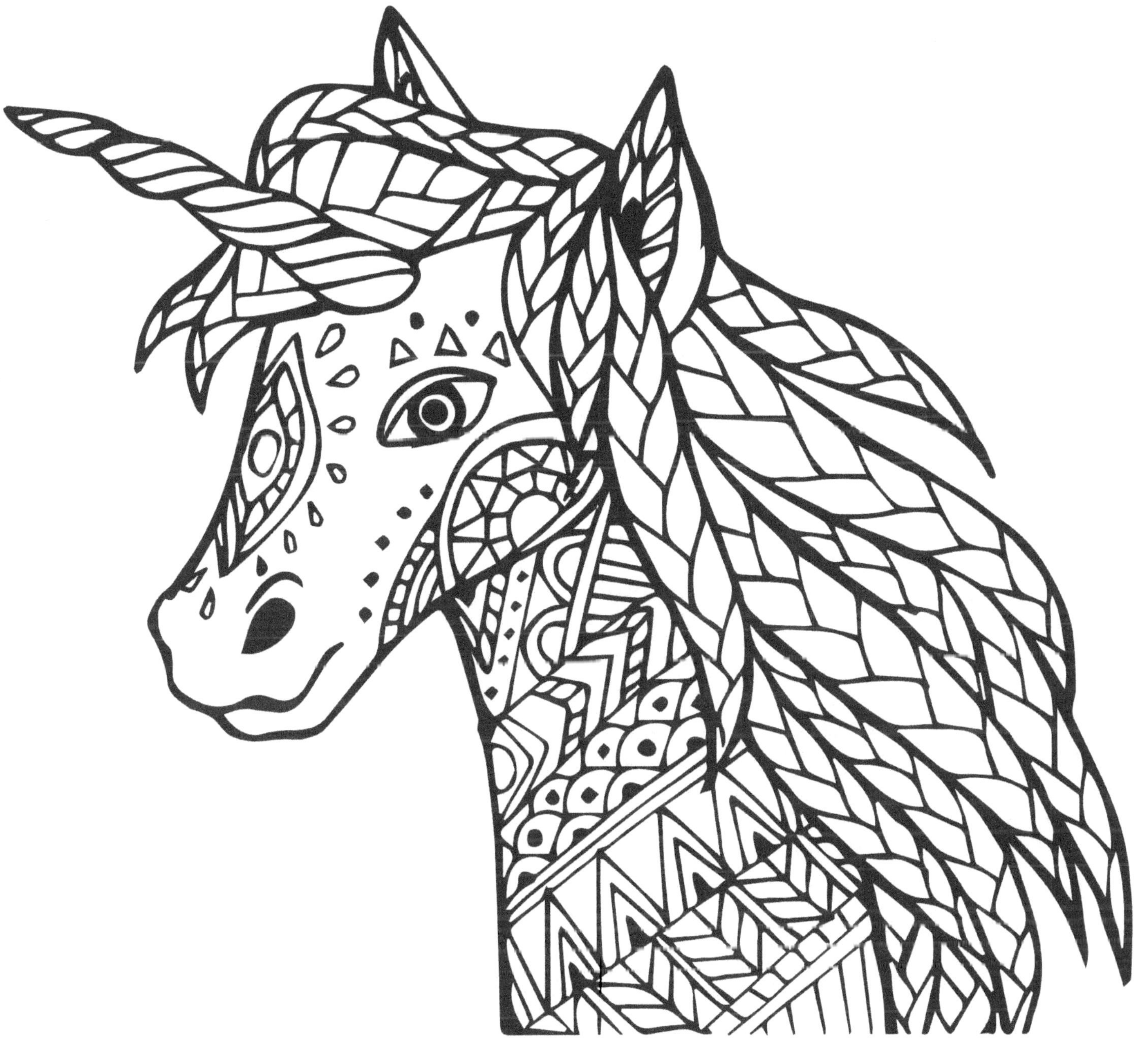

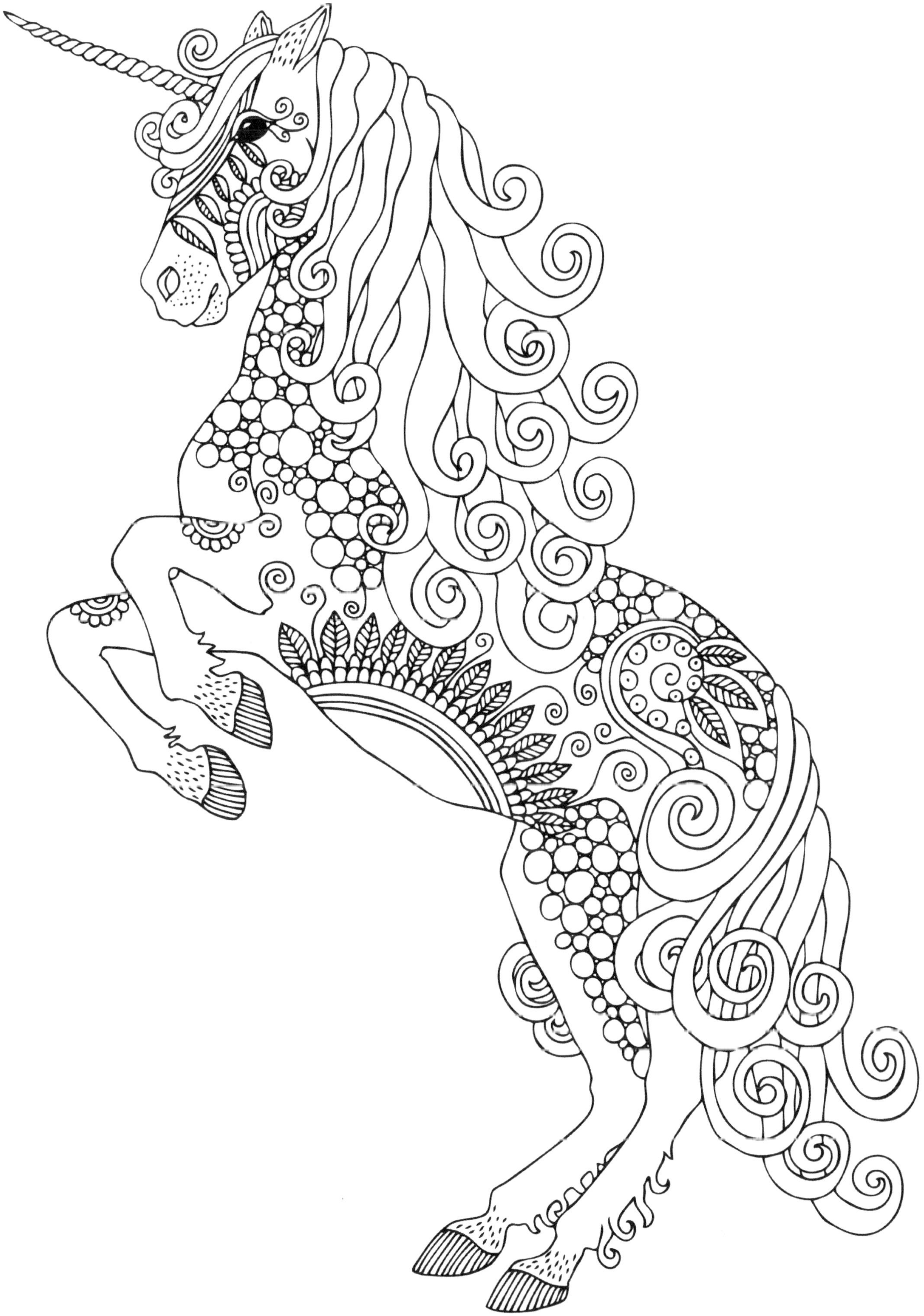

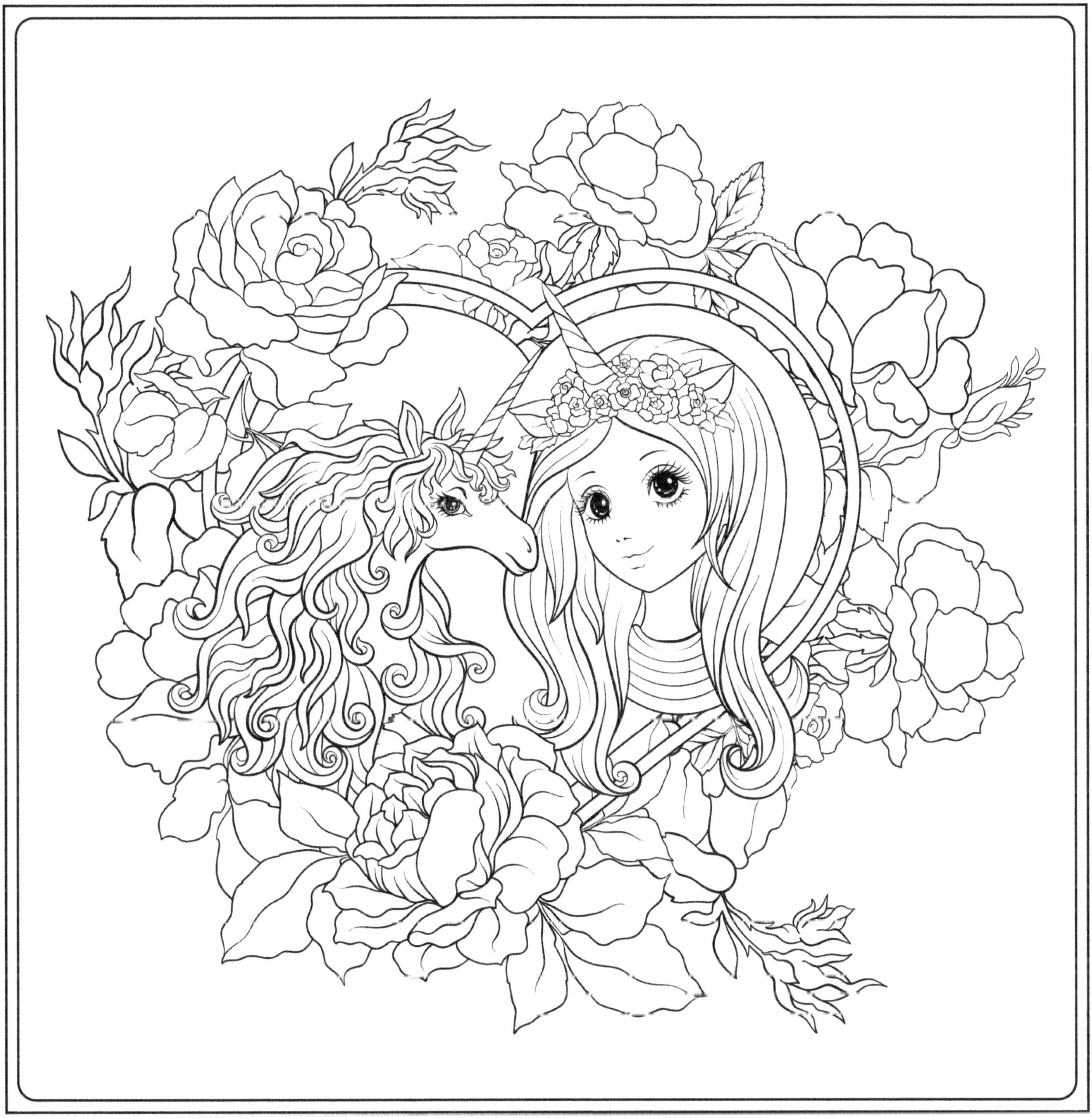

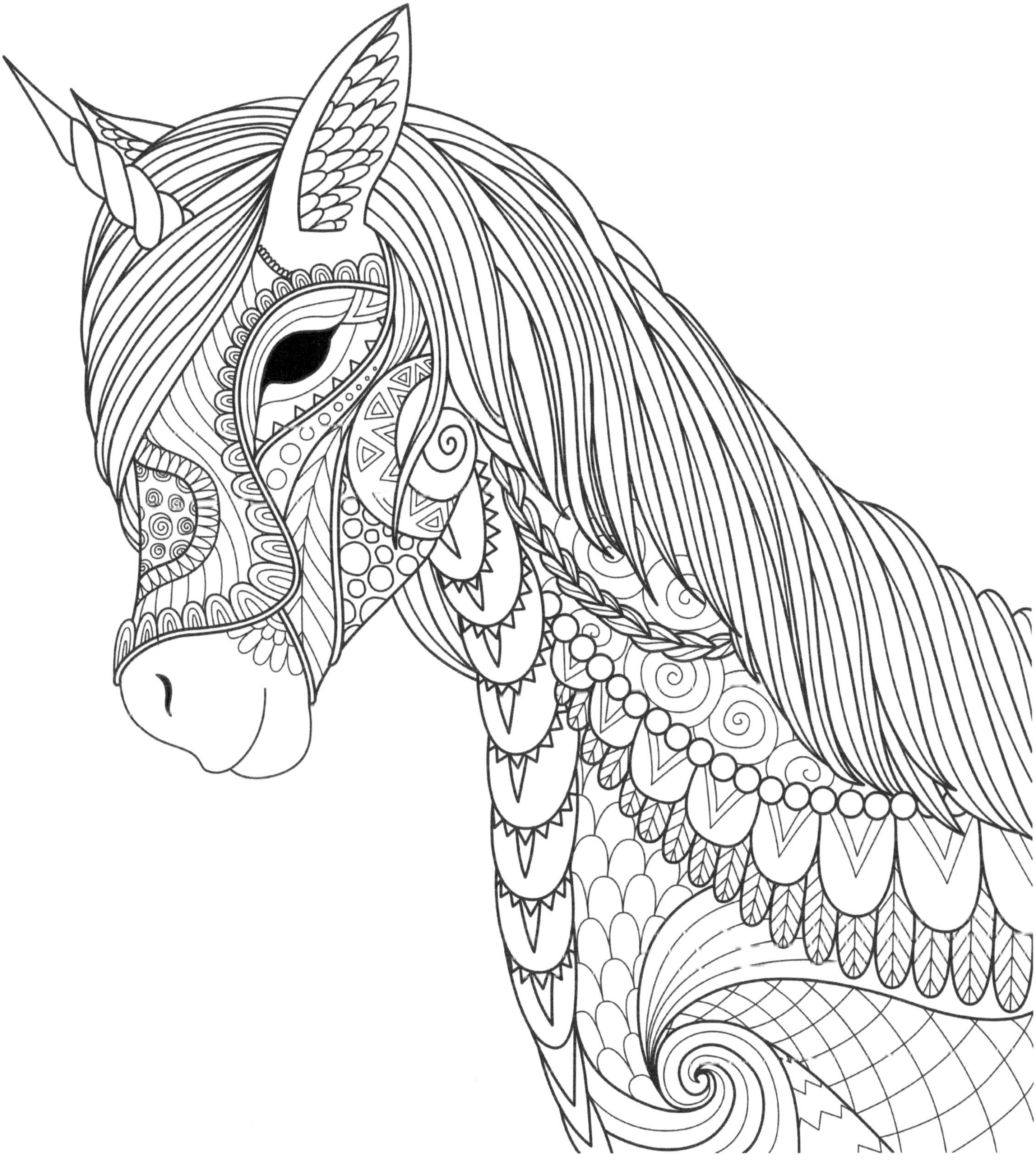

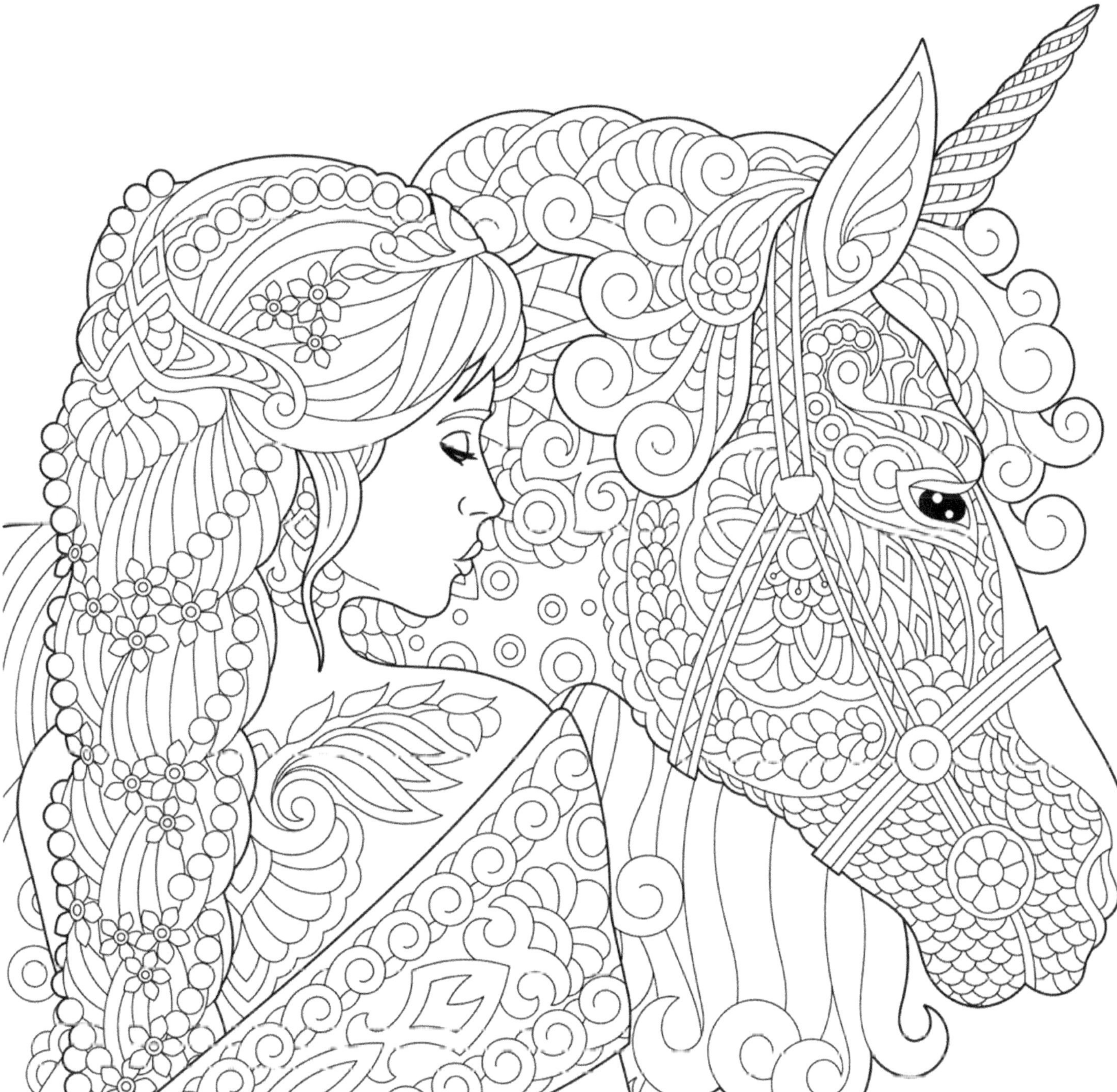

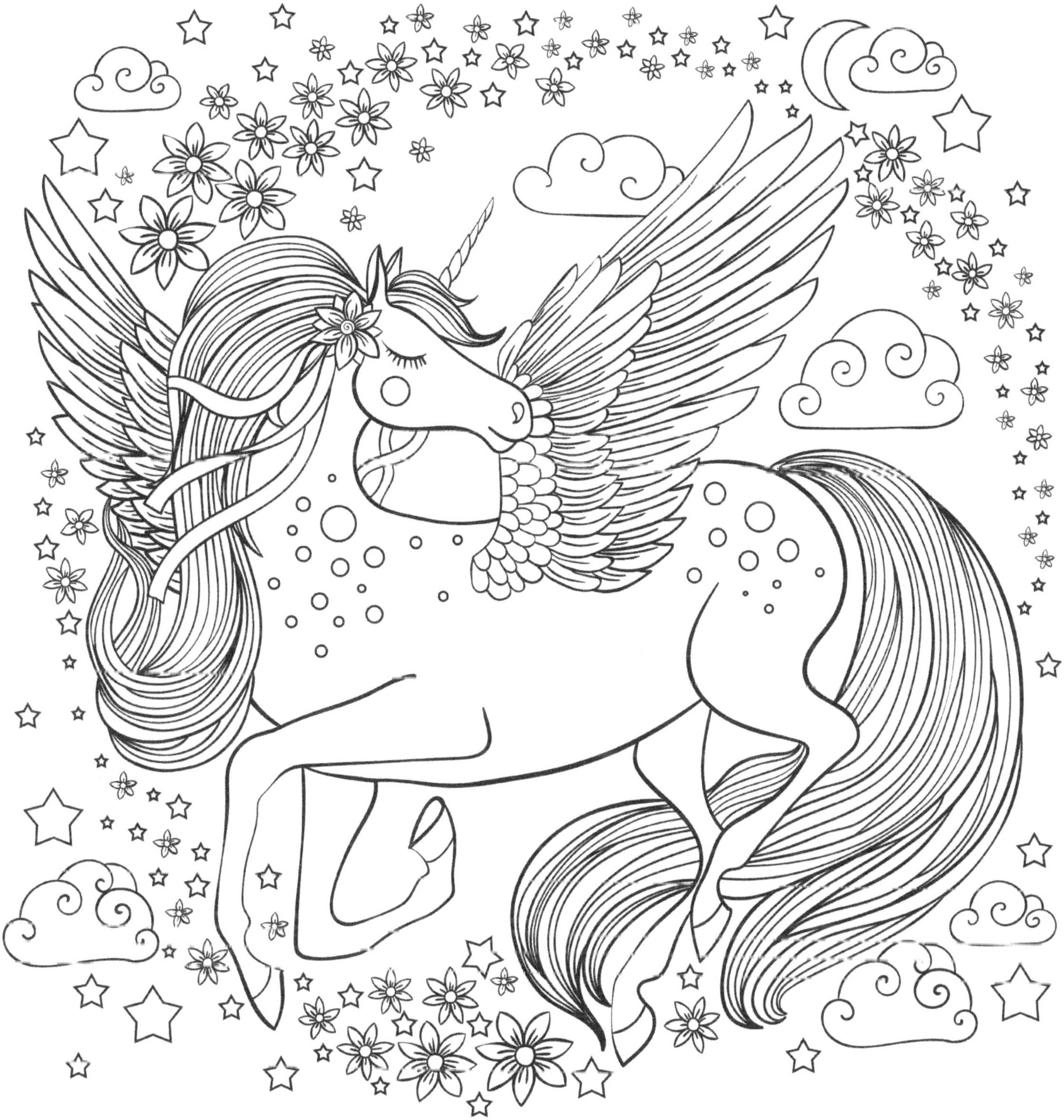

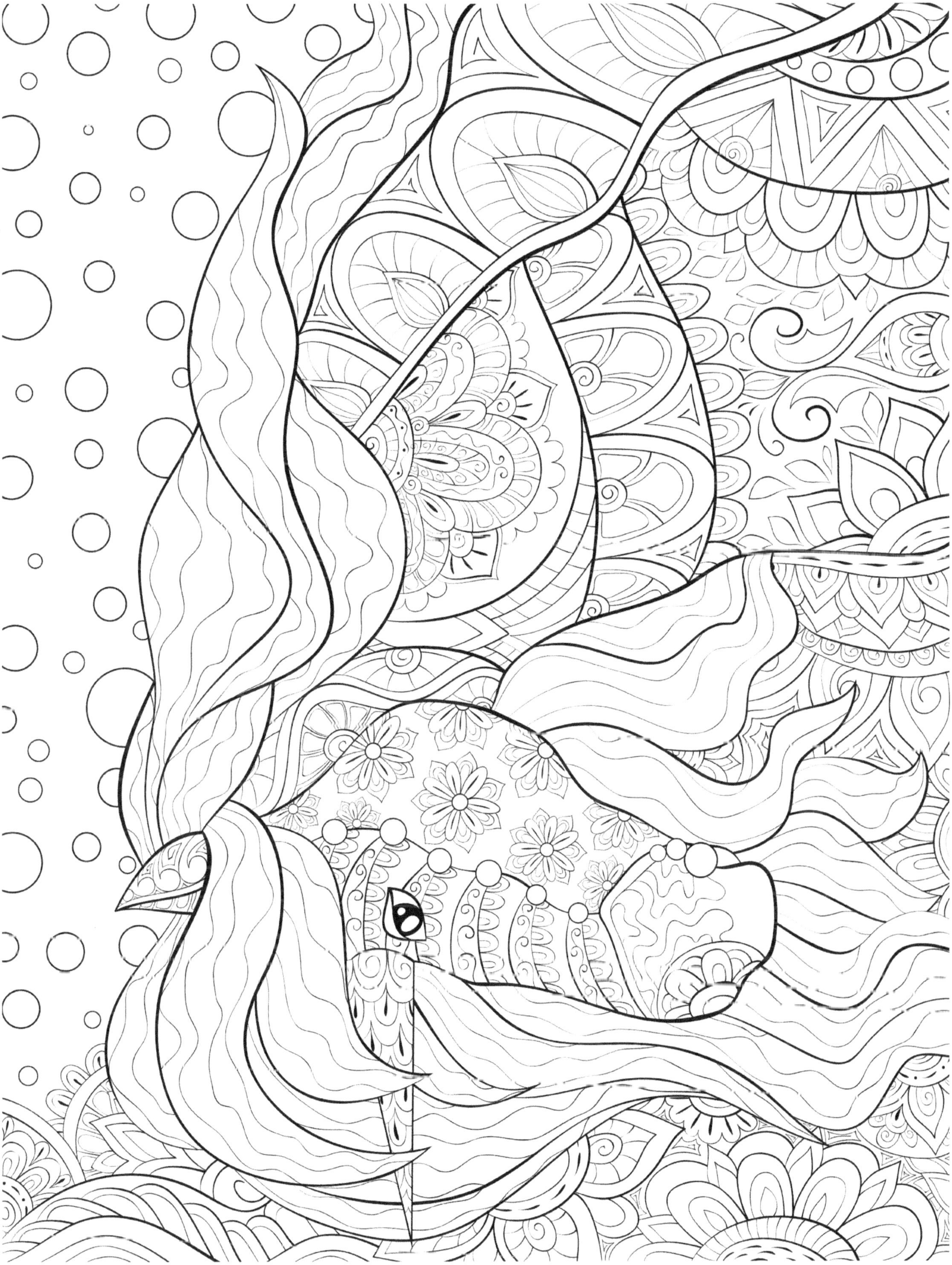

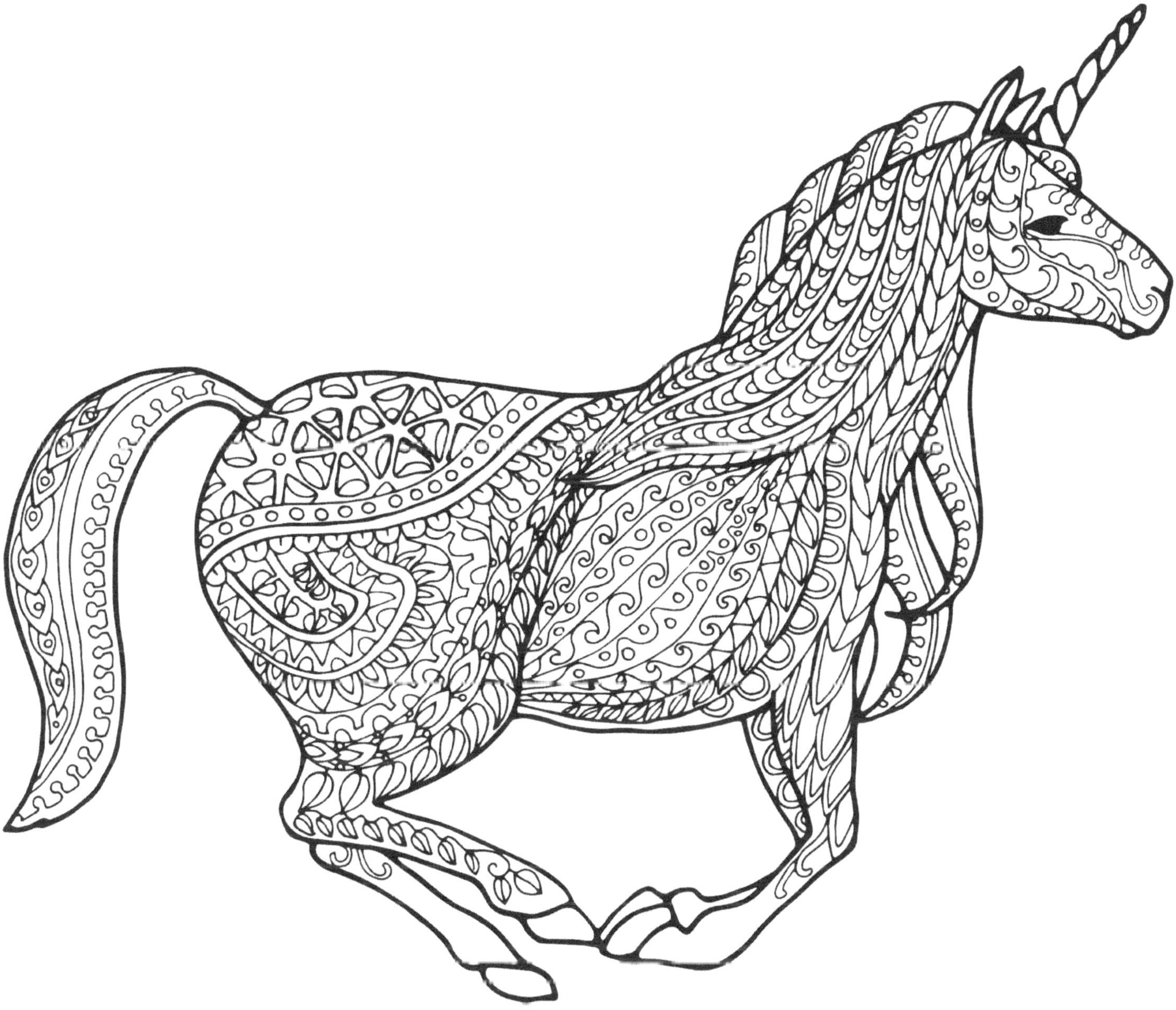

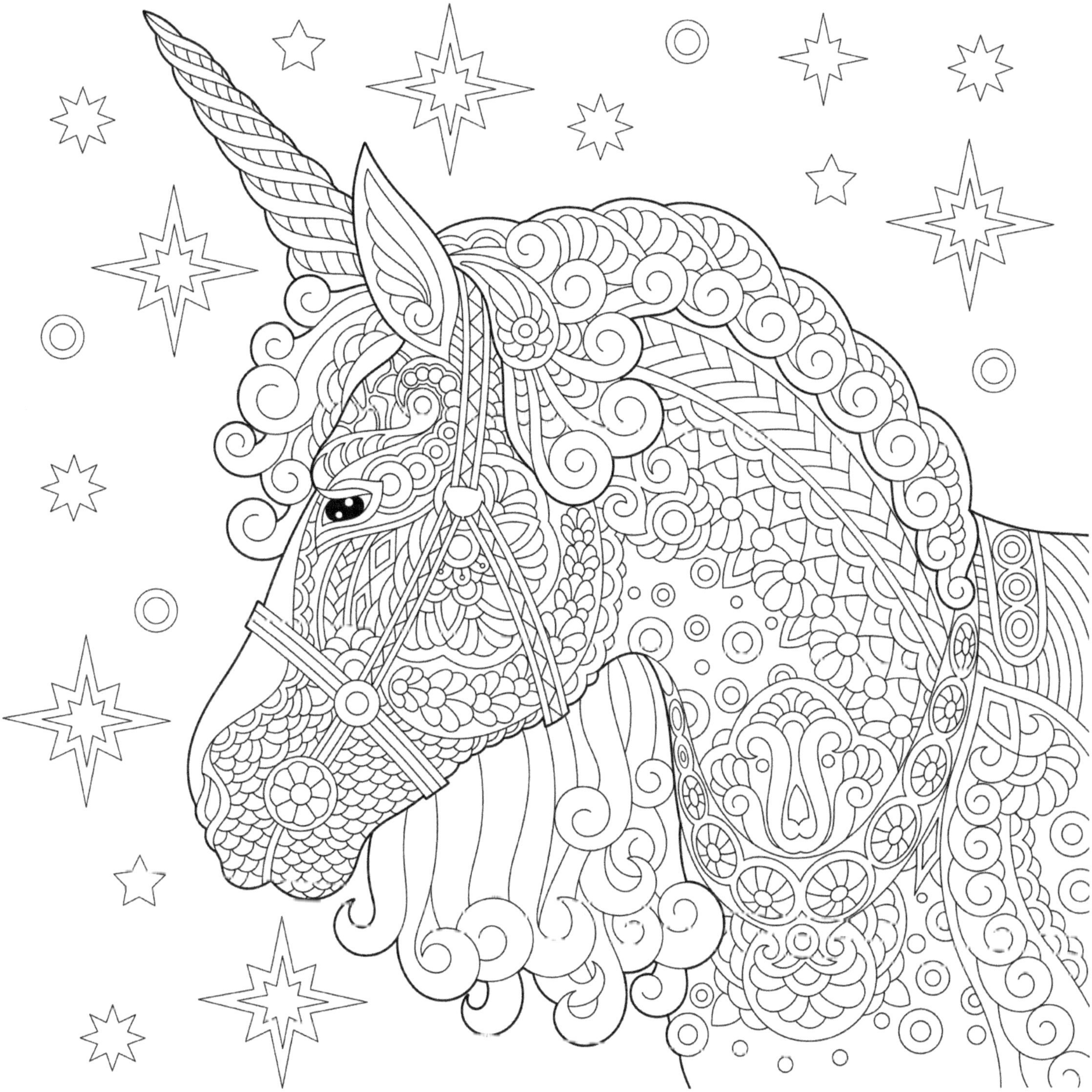

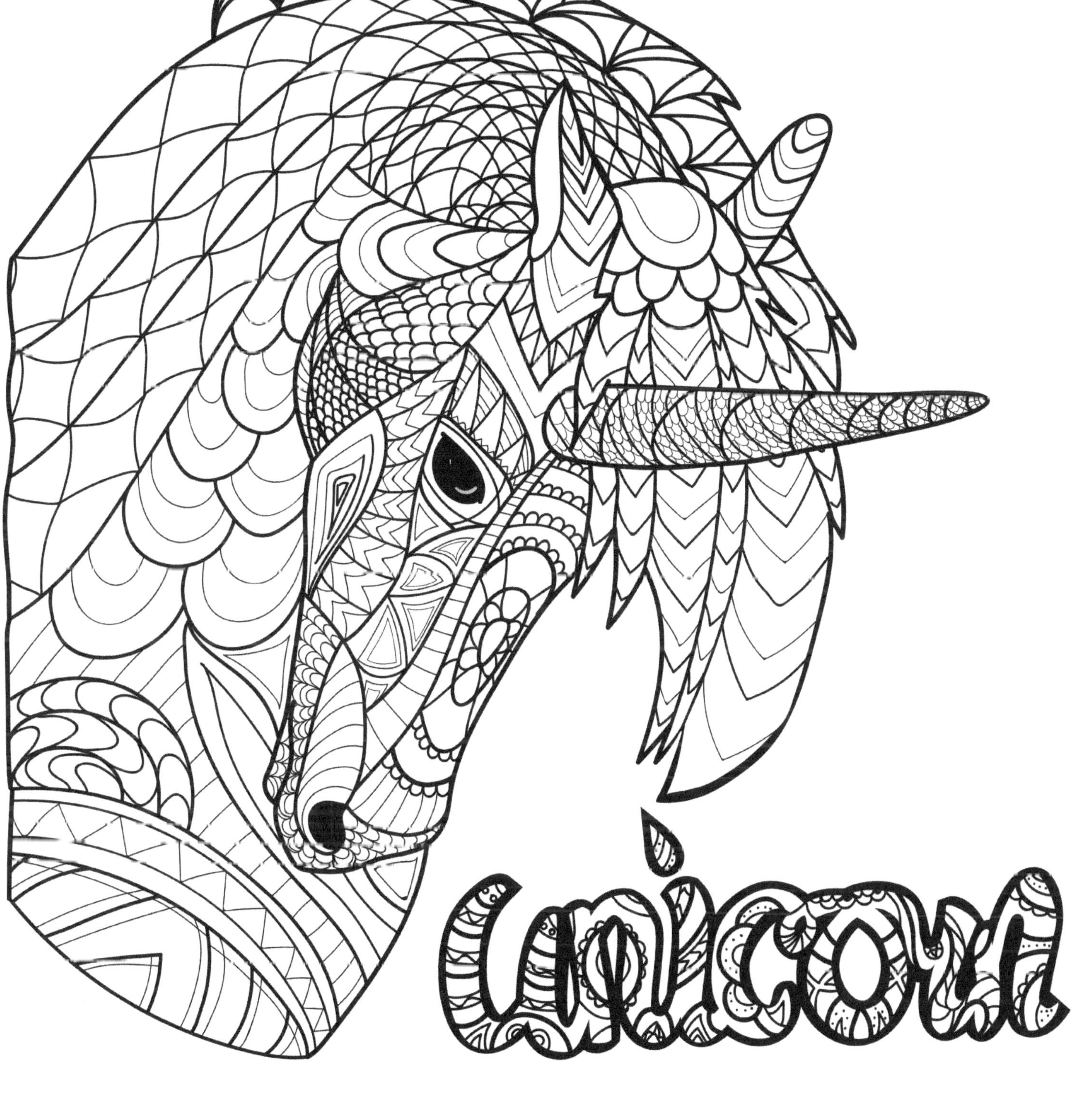
Unicorn

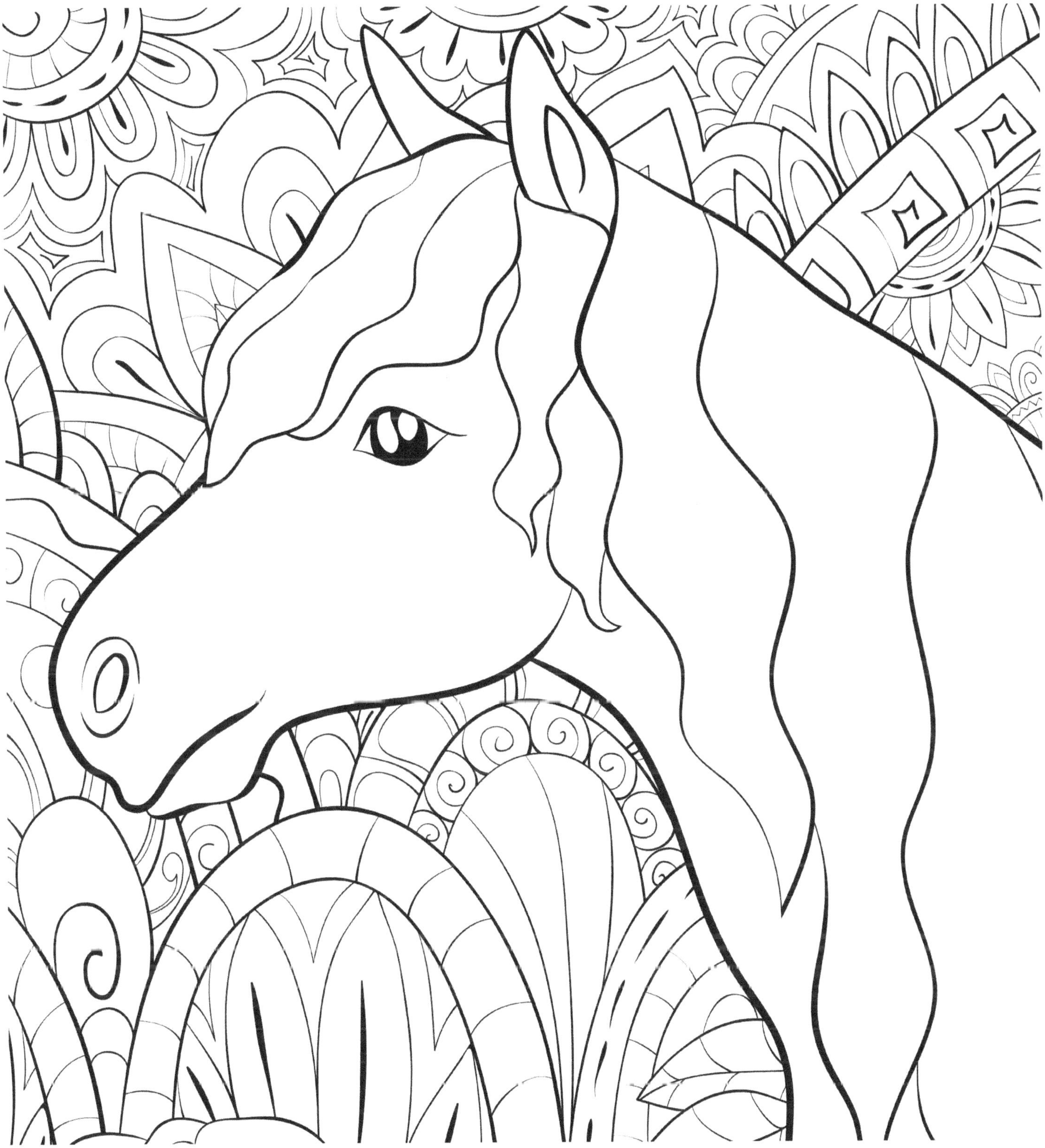

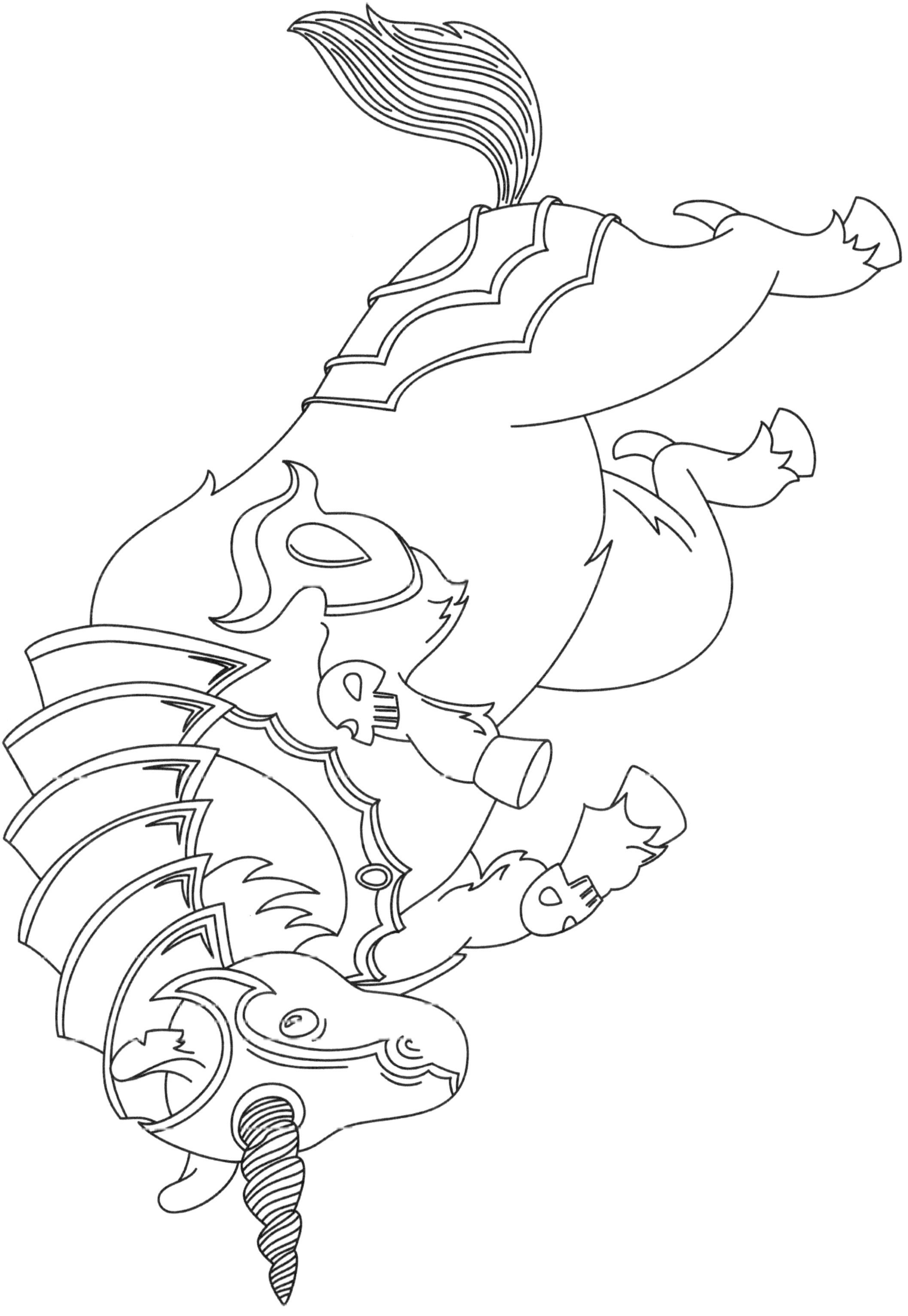

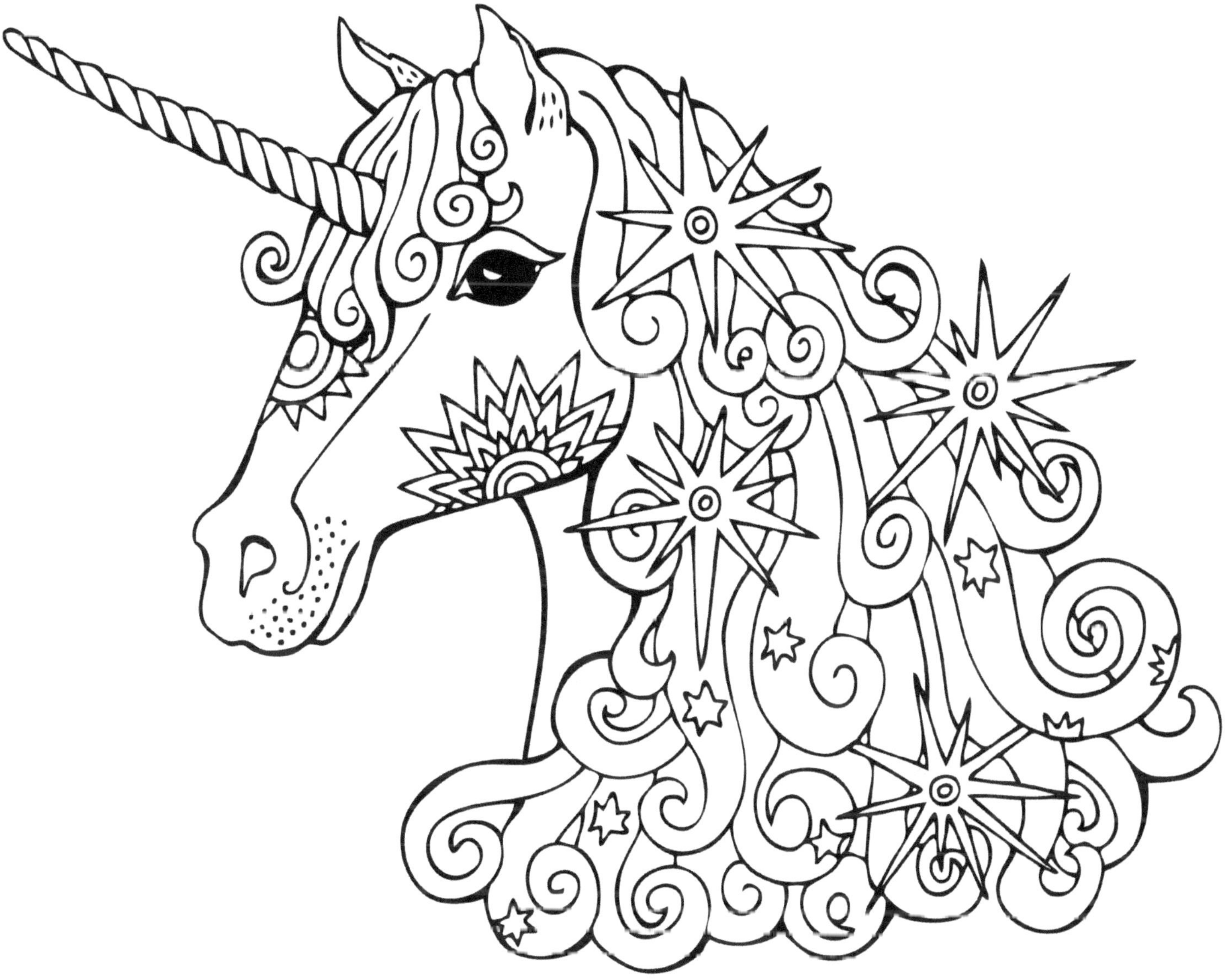

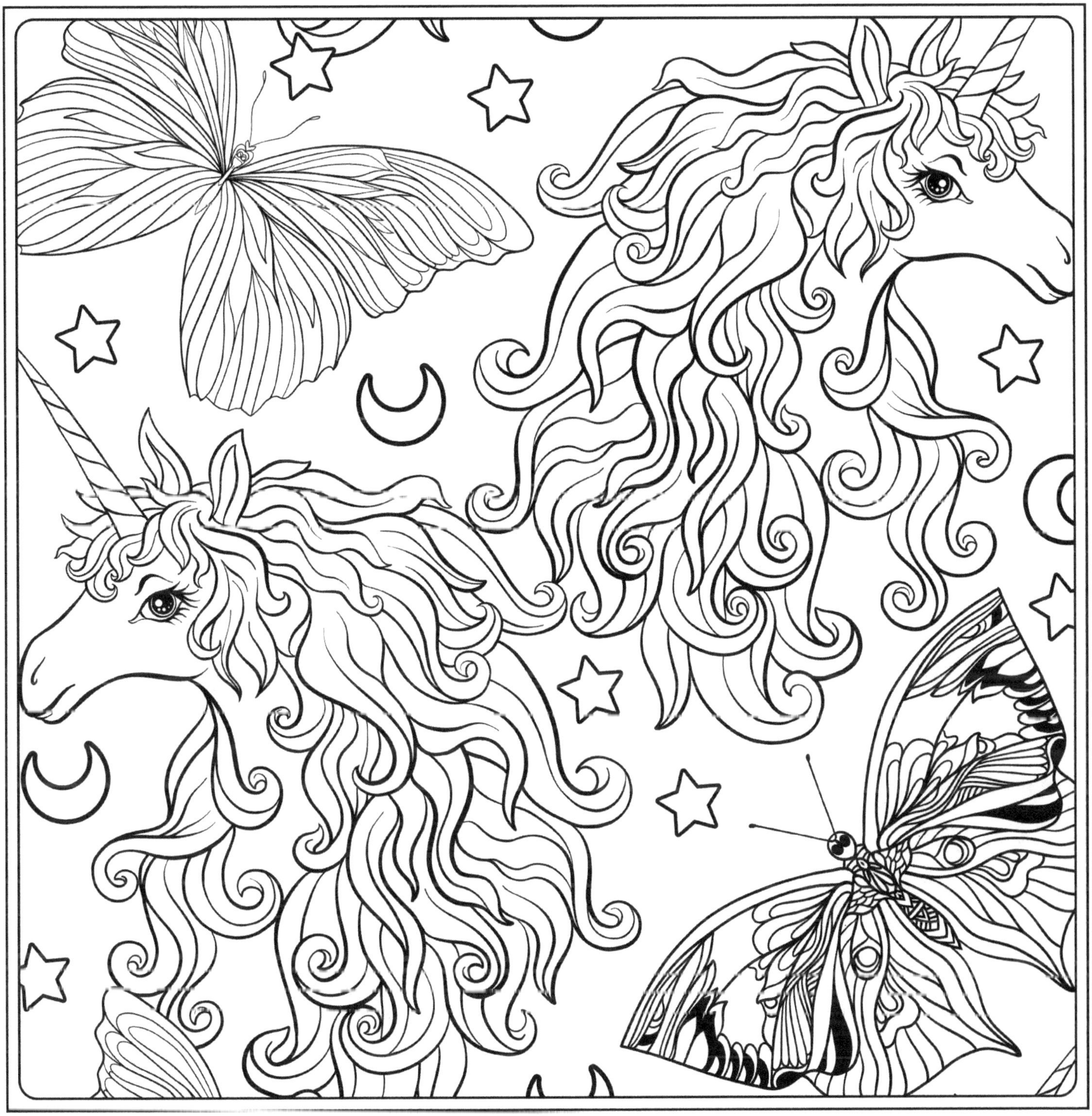

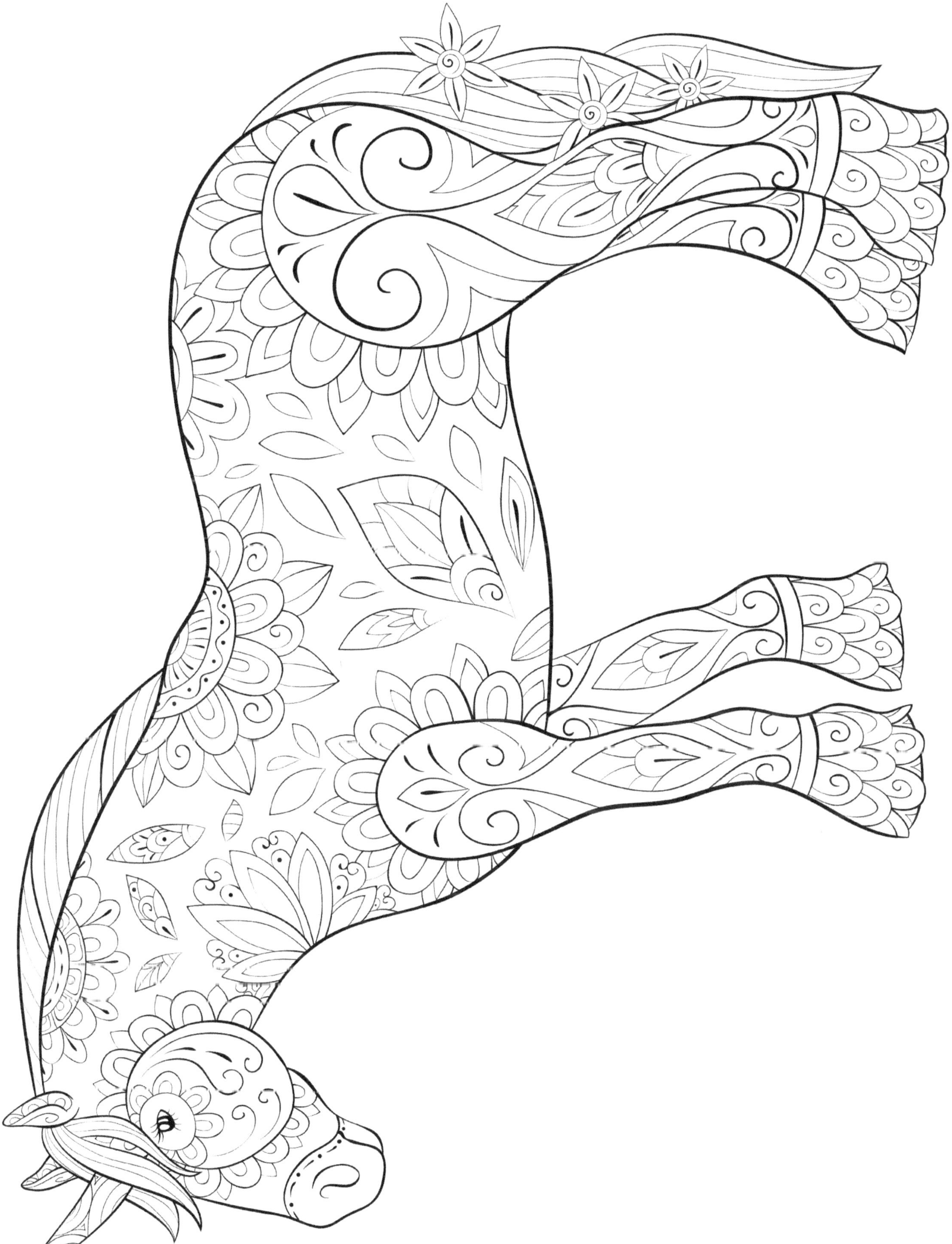

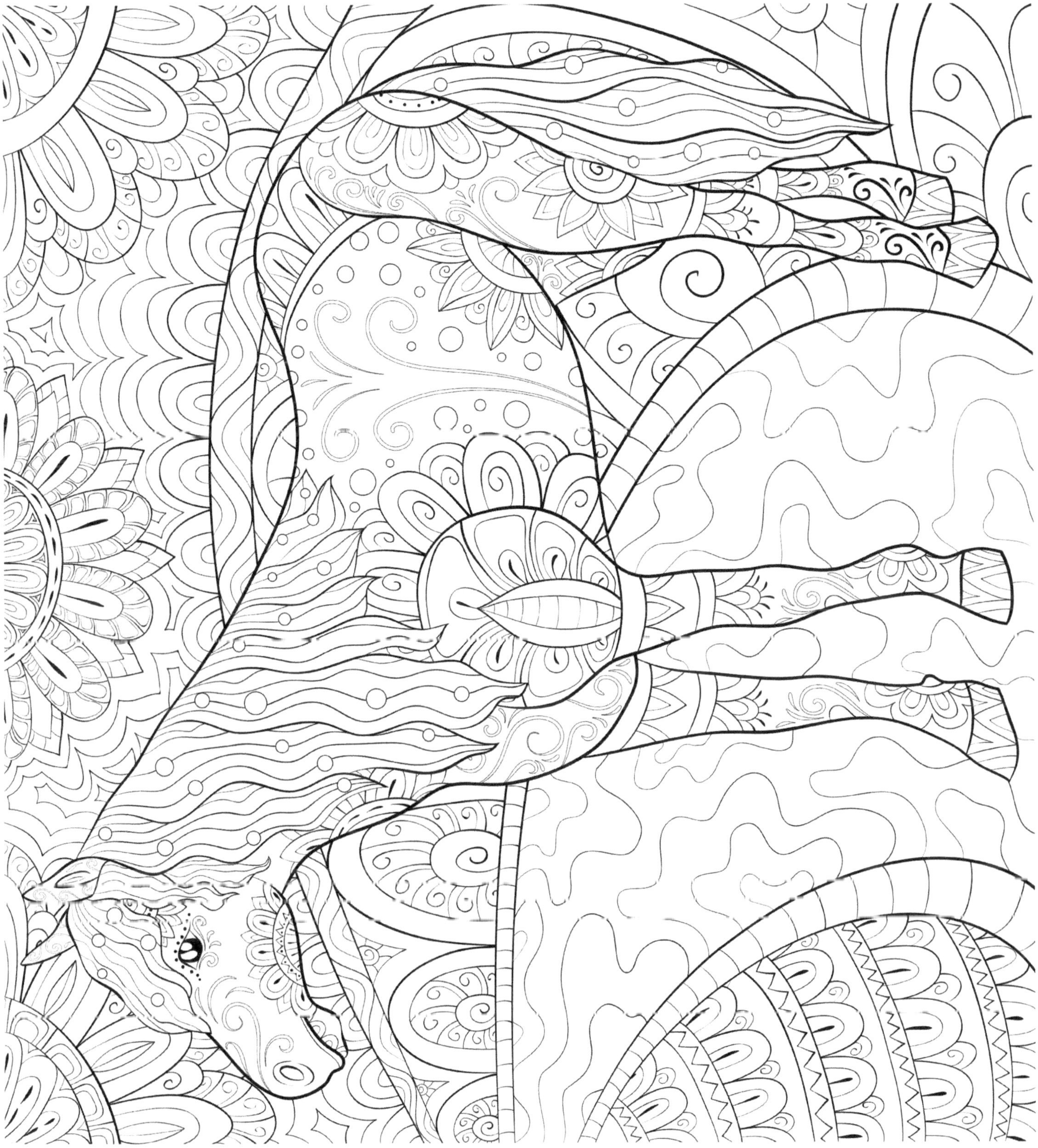

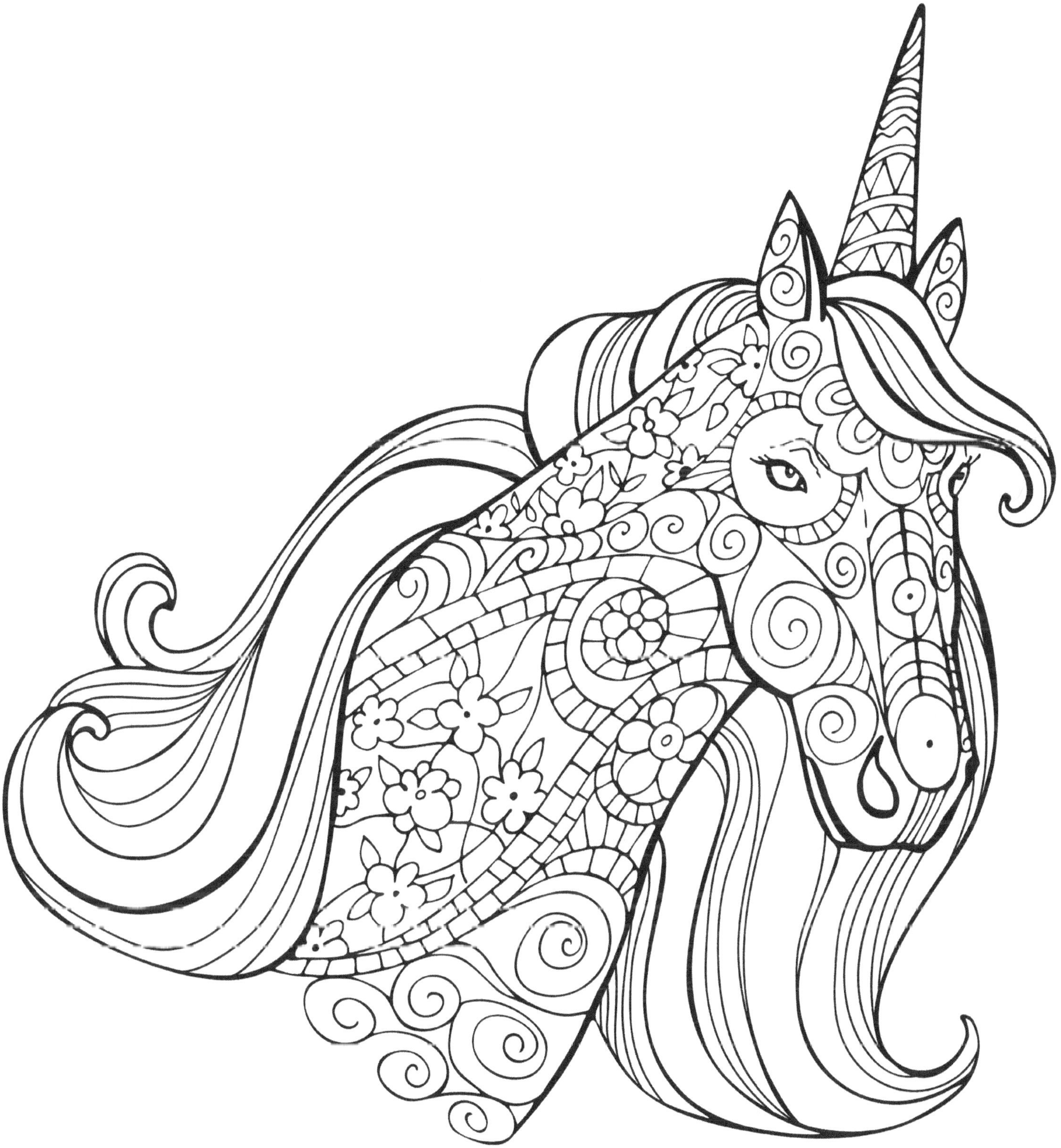

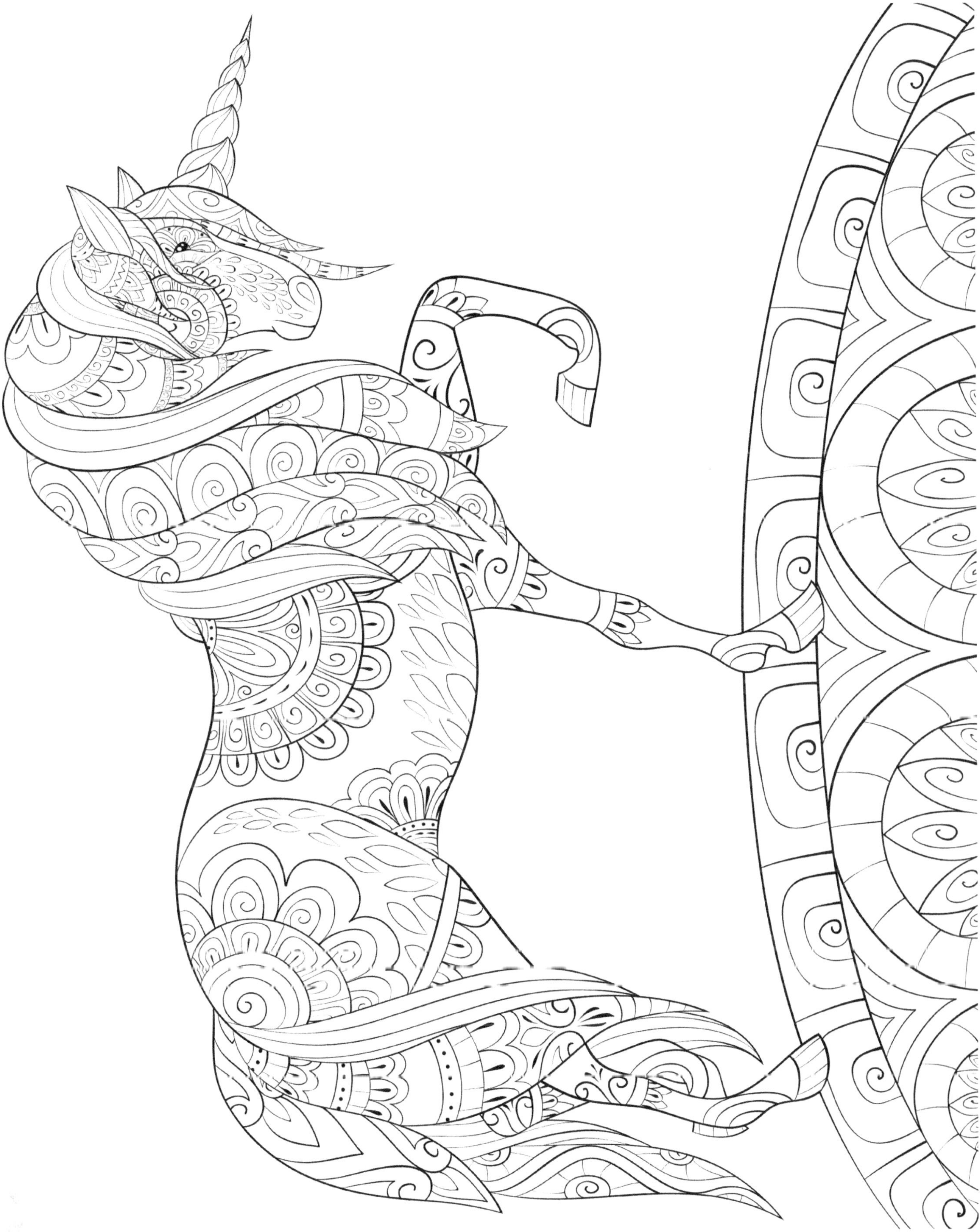

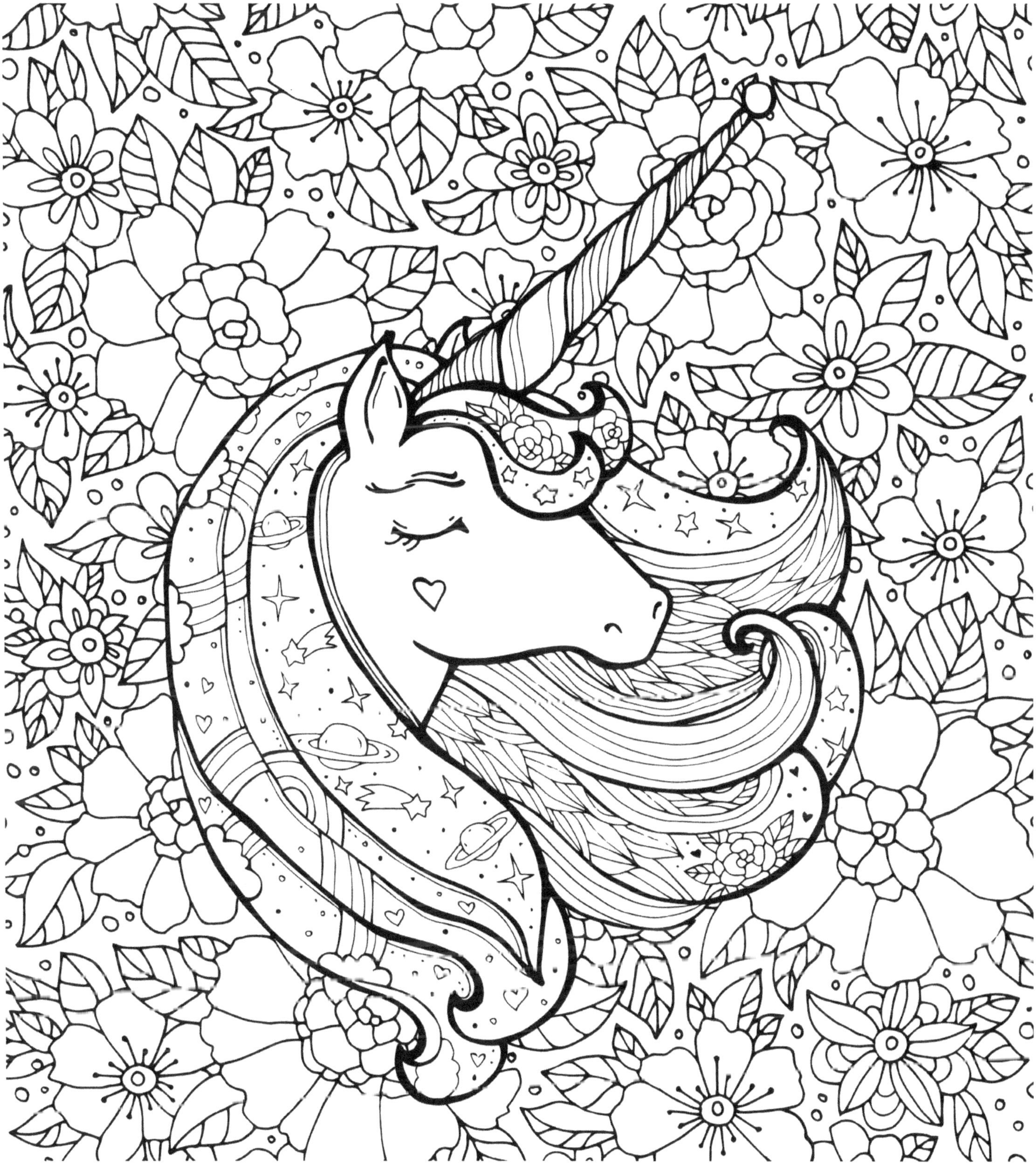

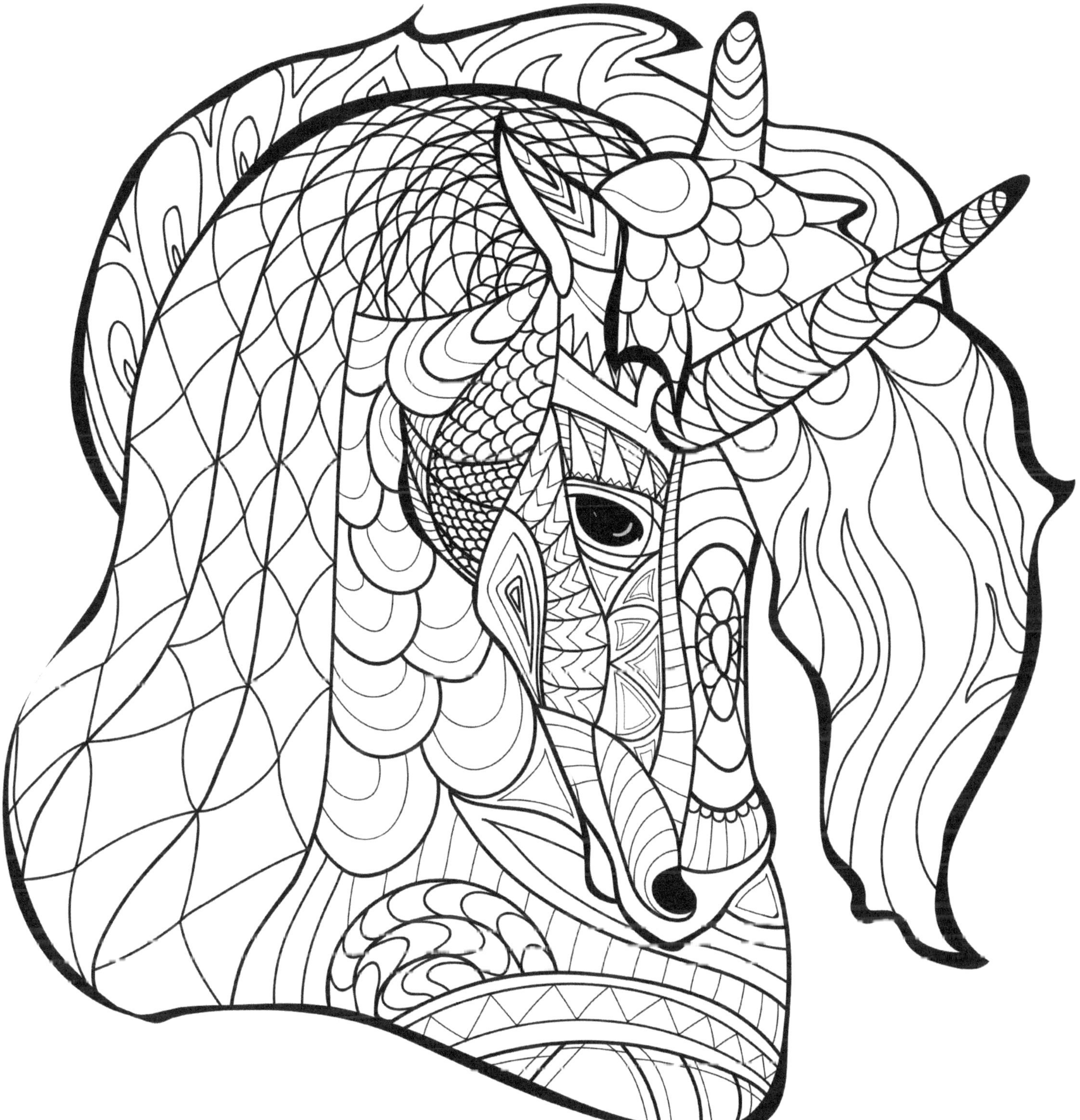

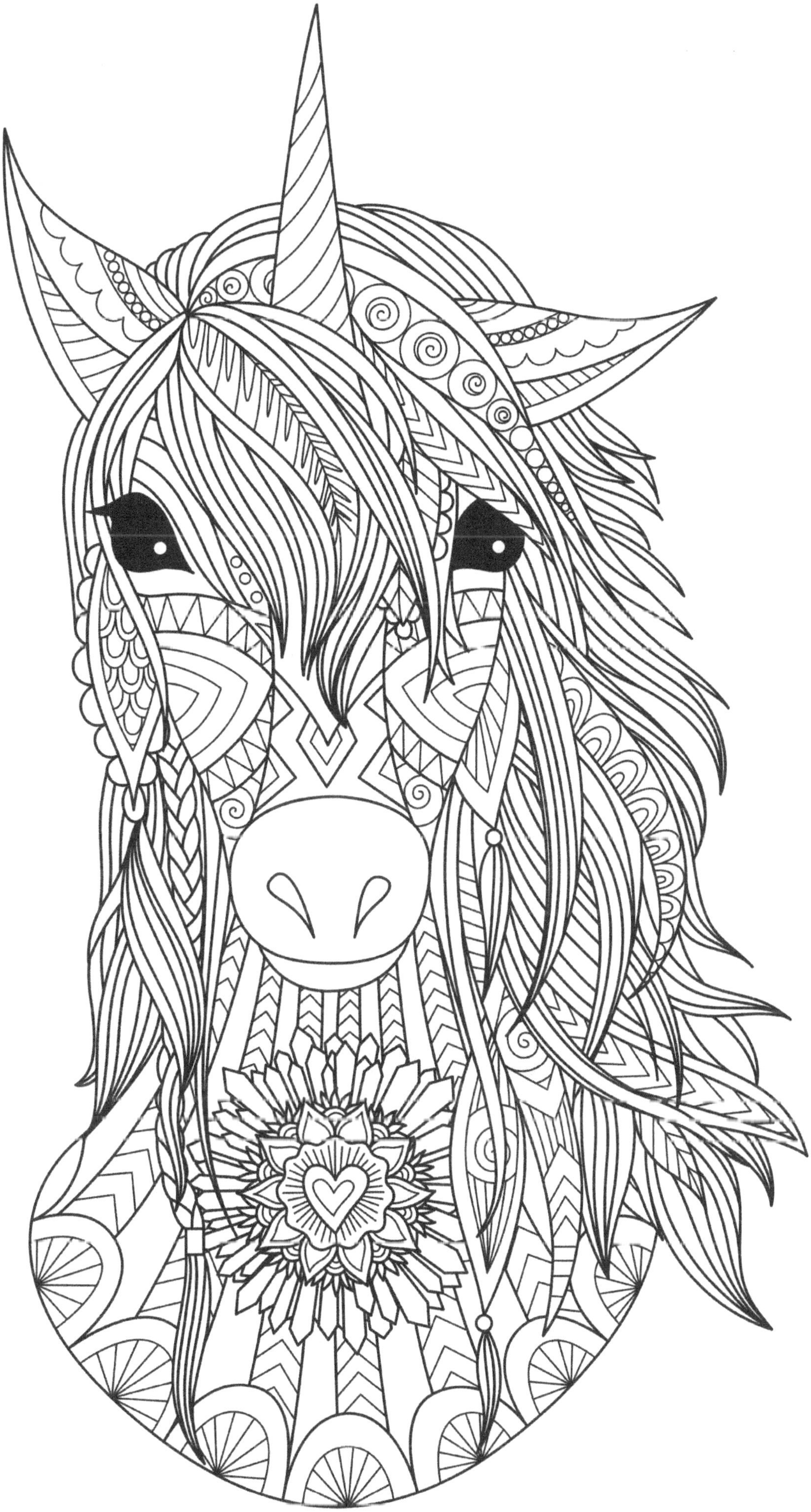

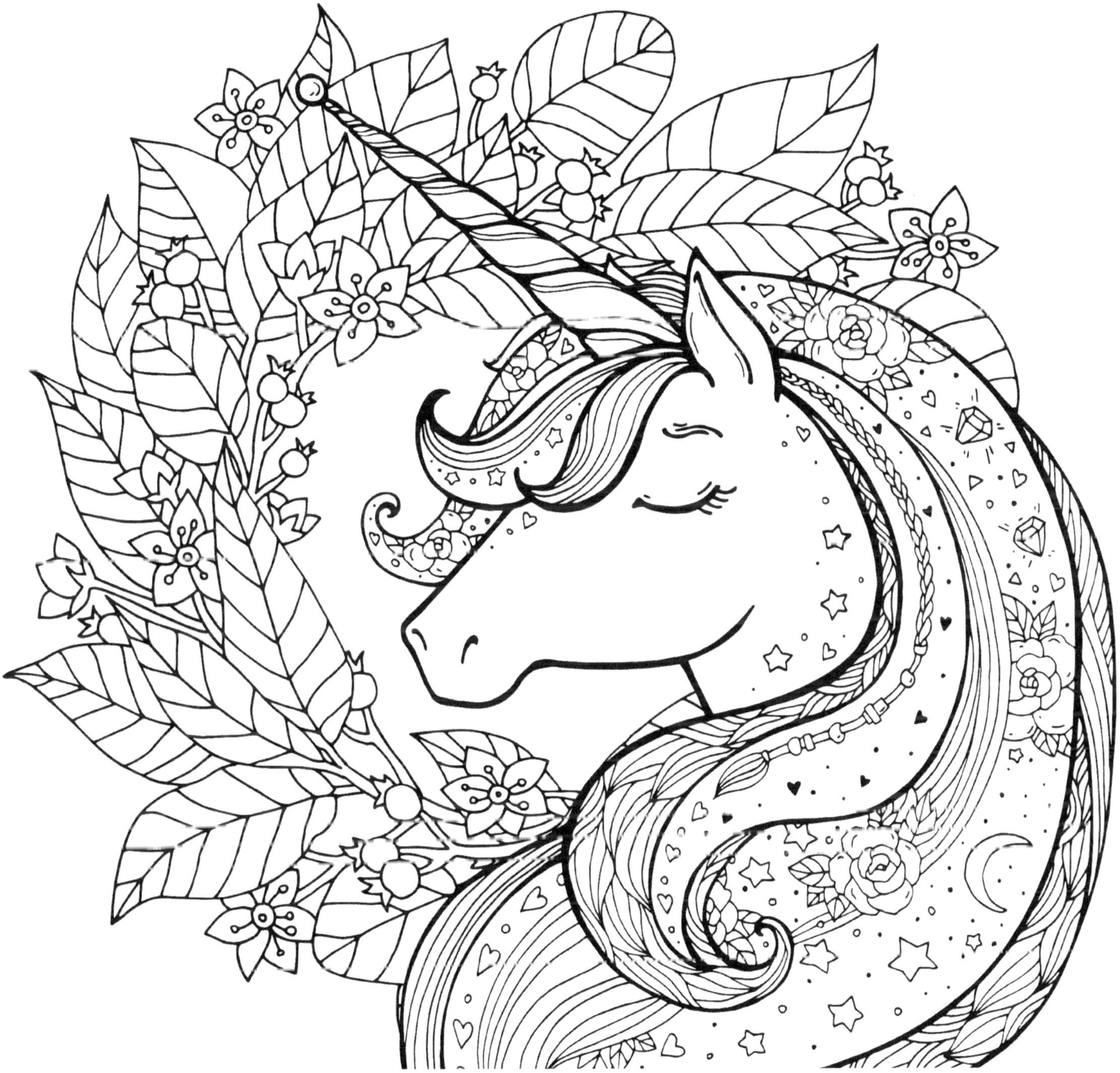

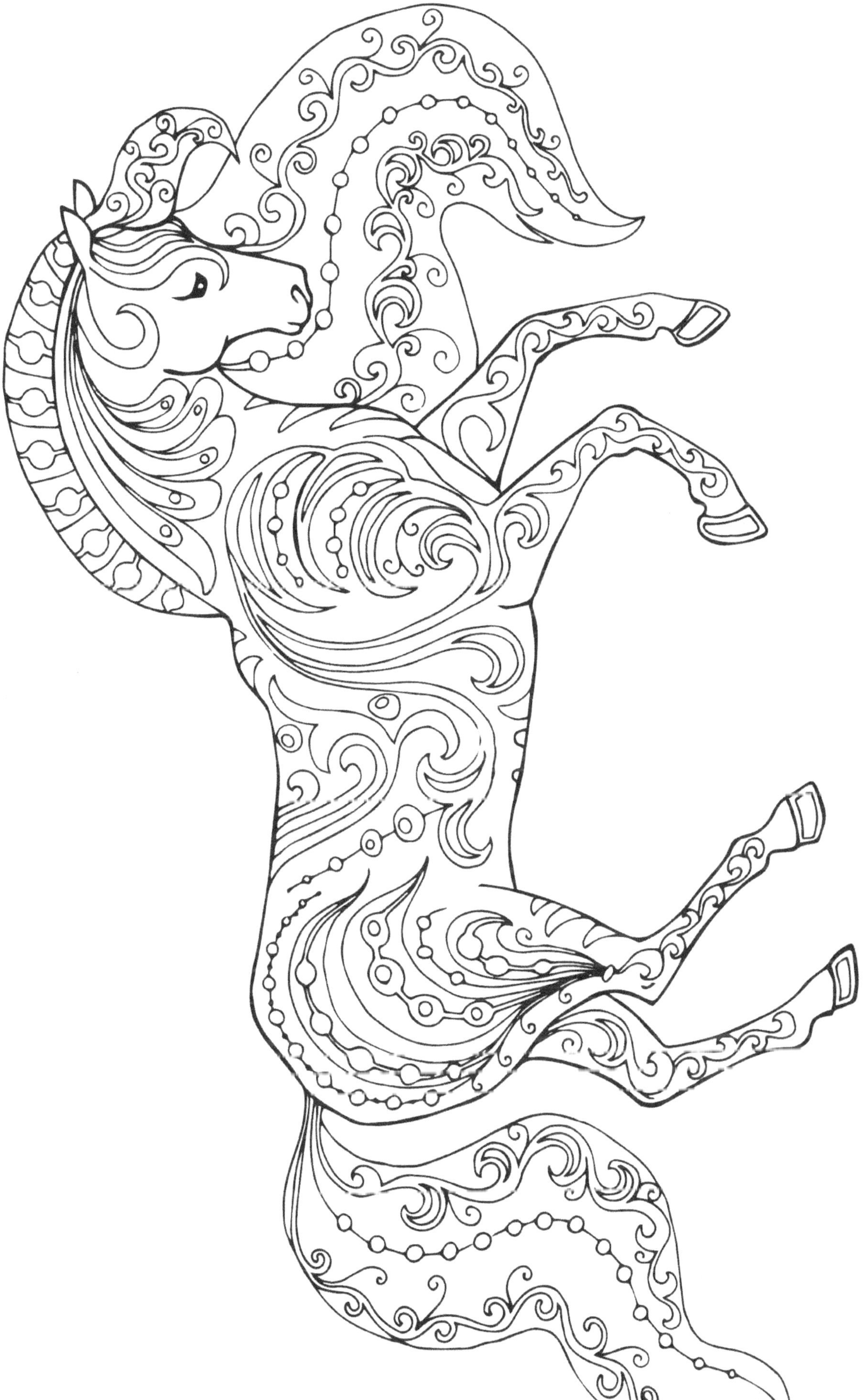

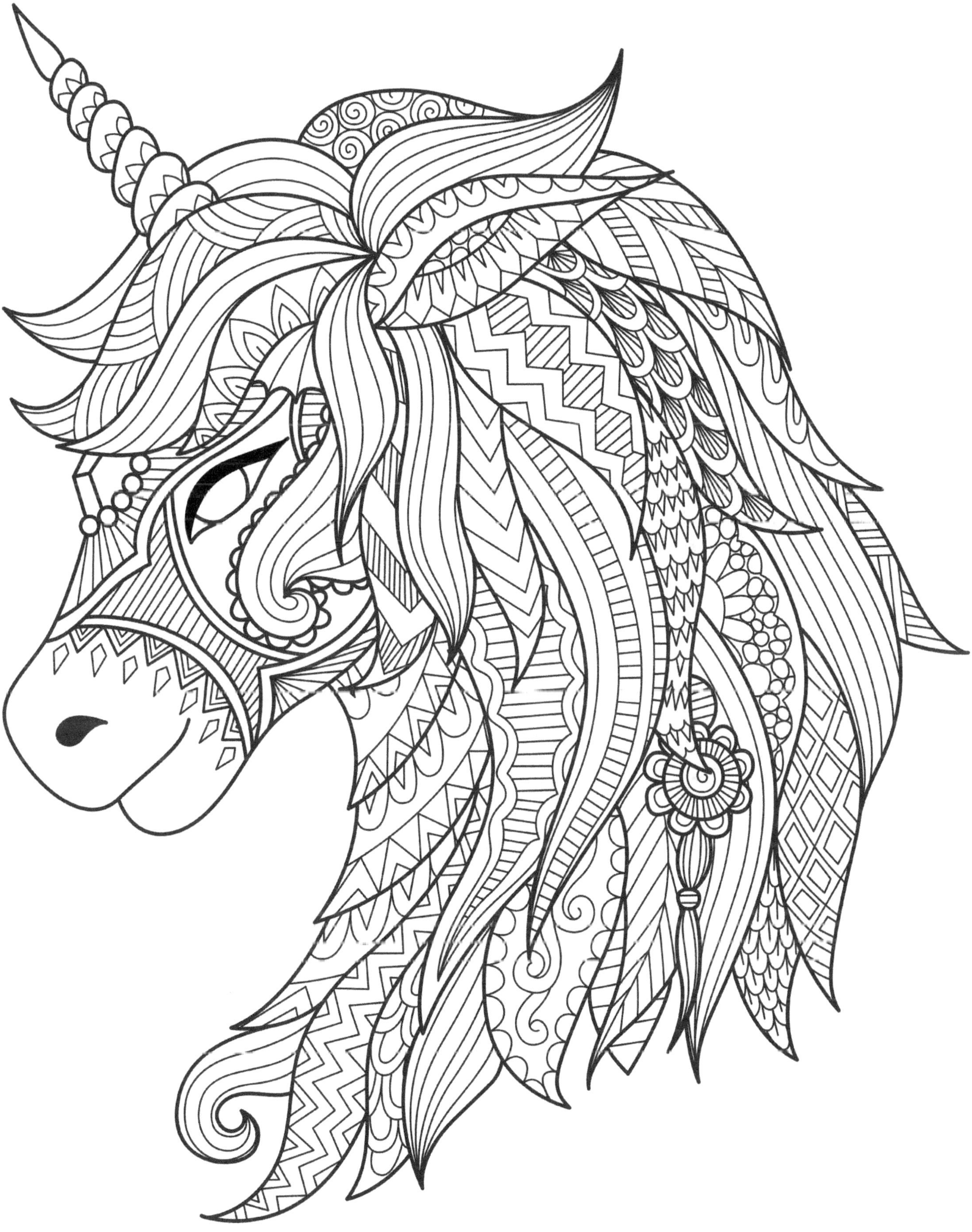

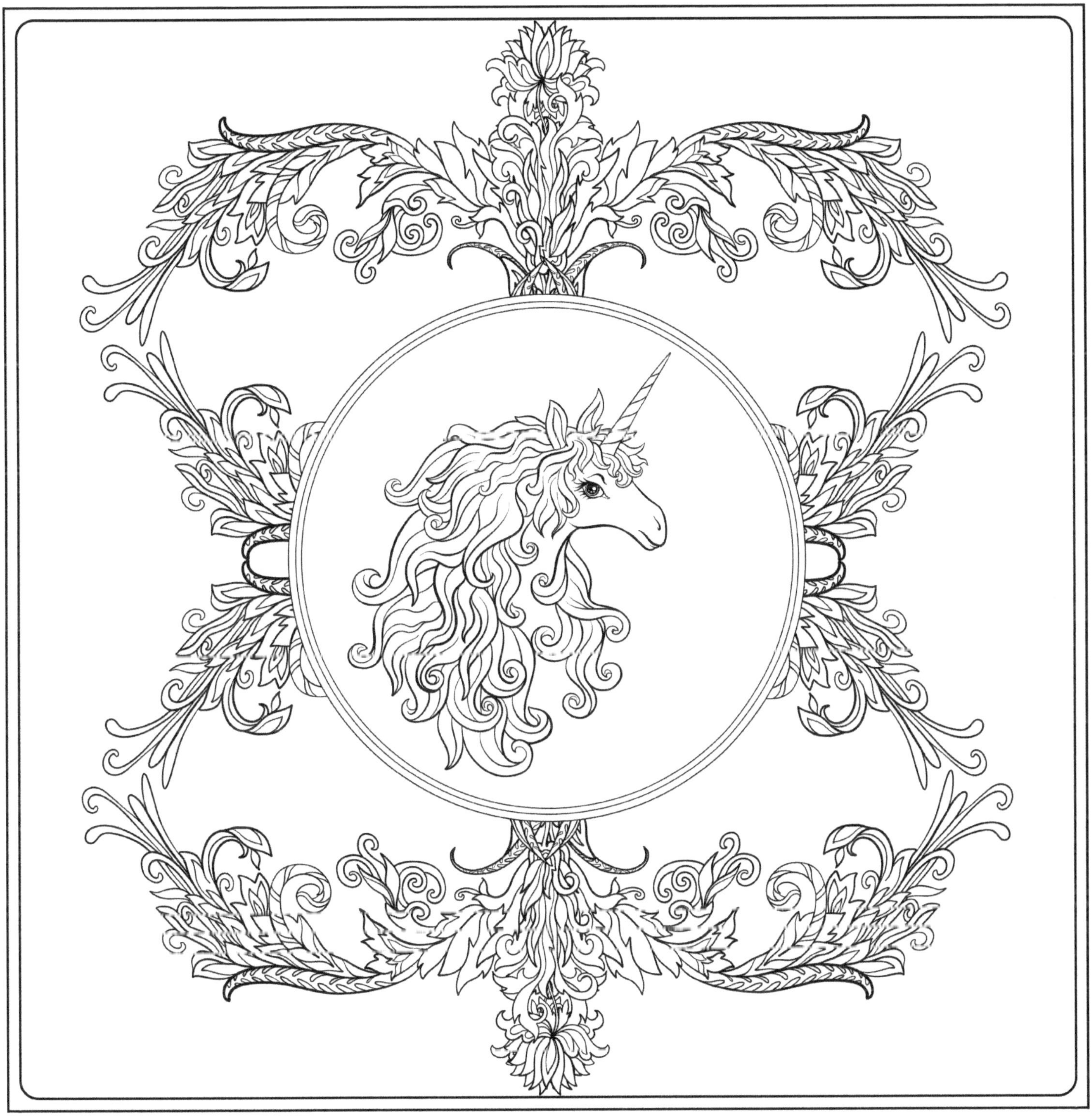

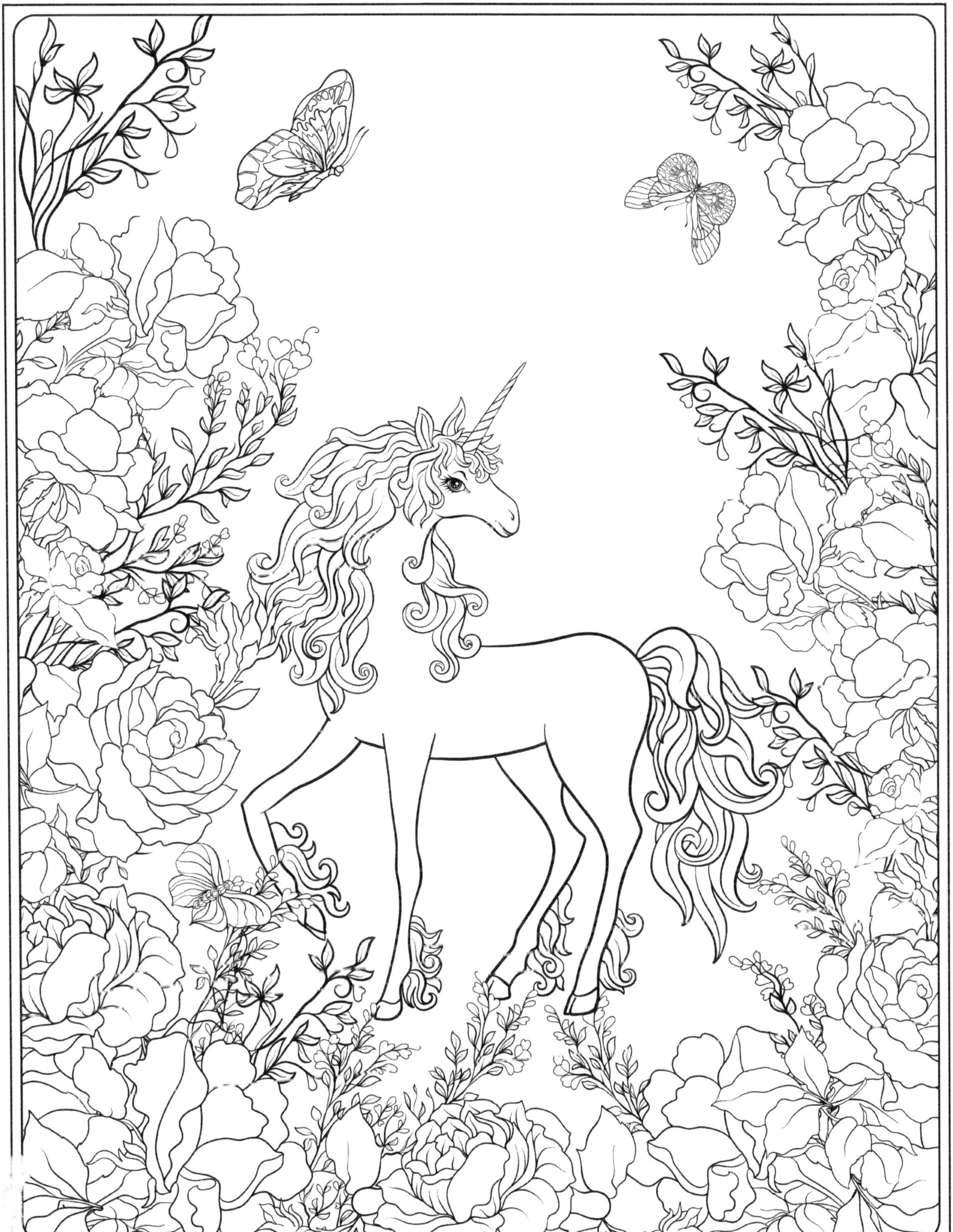

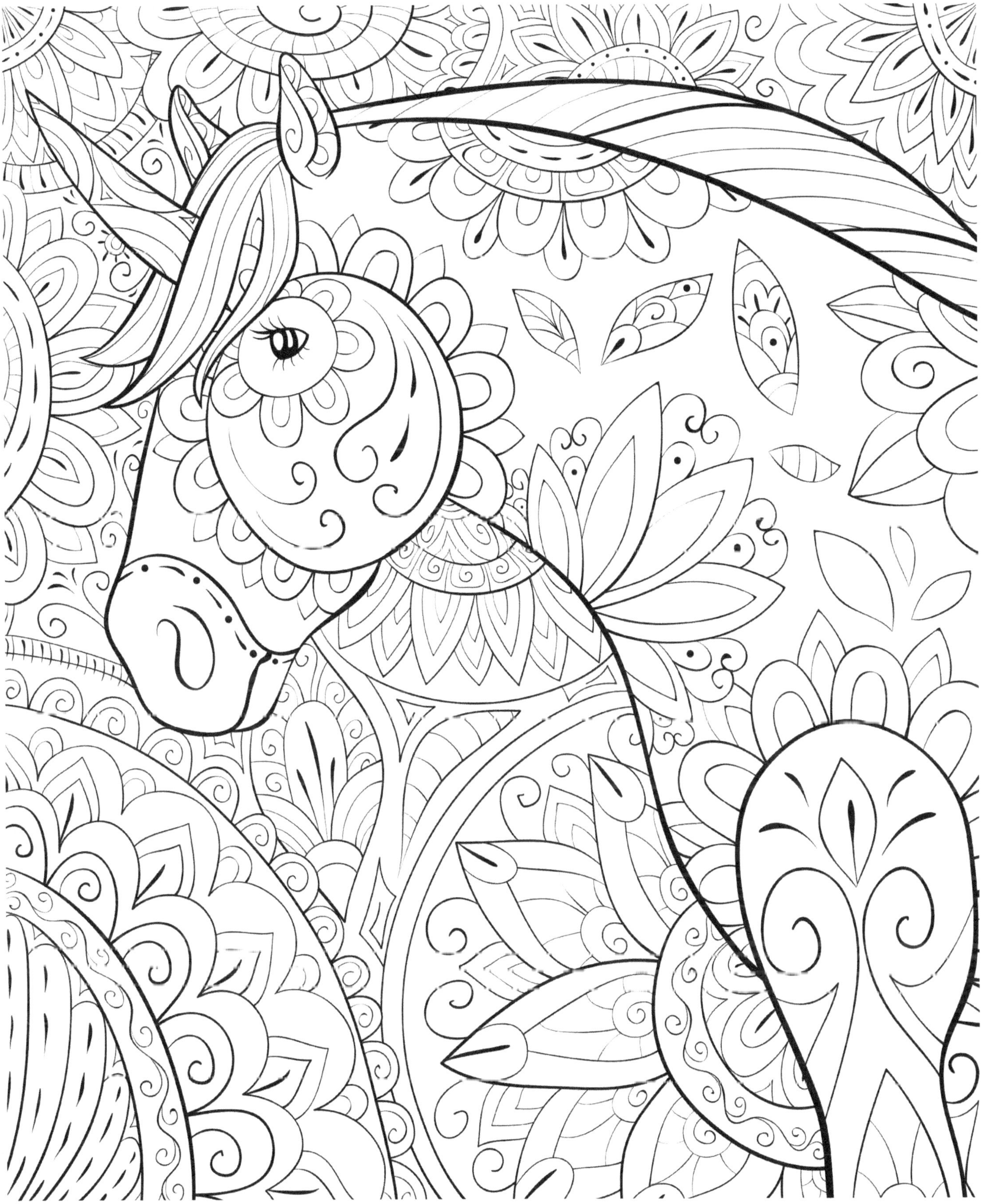

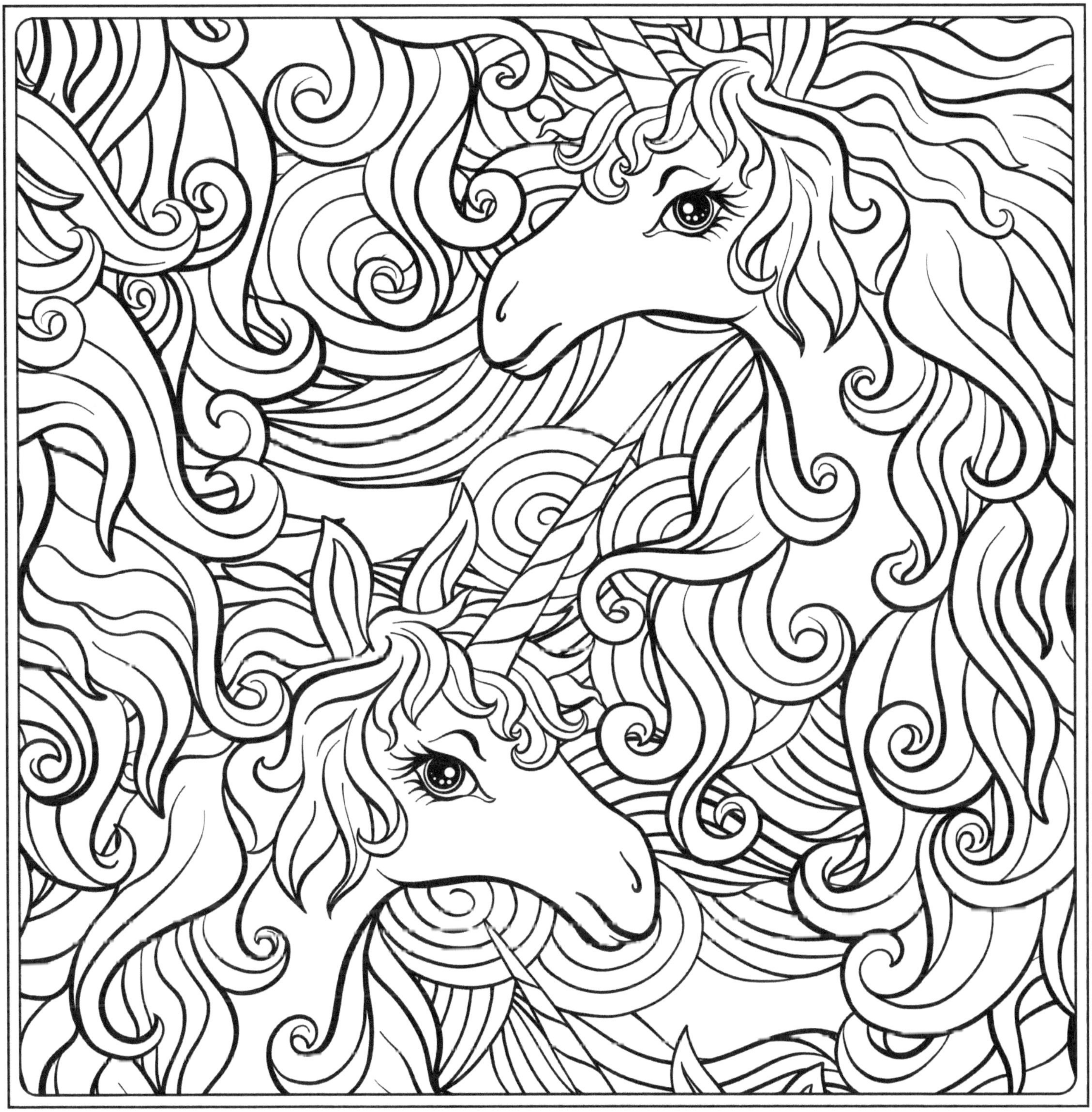

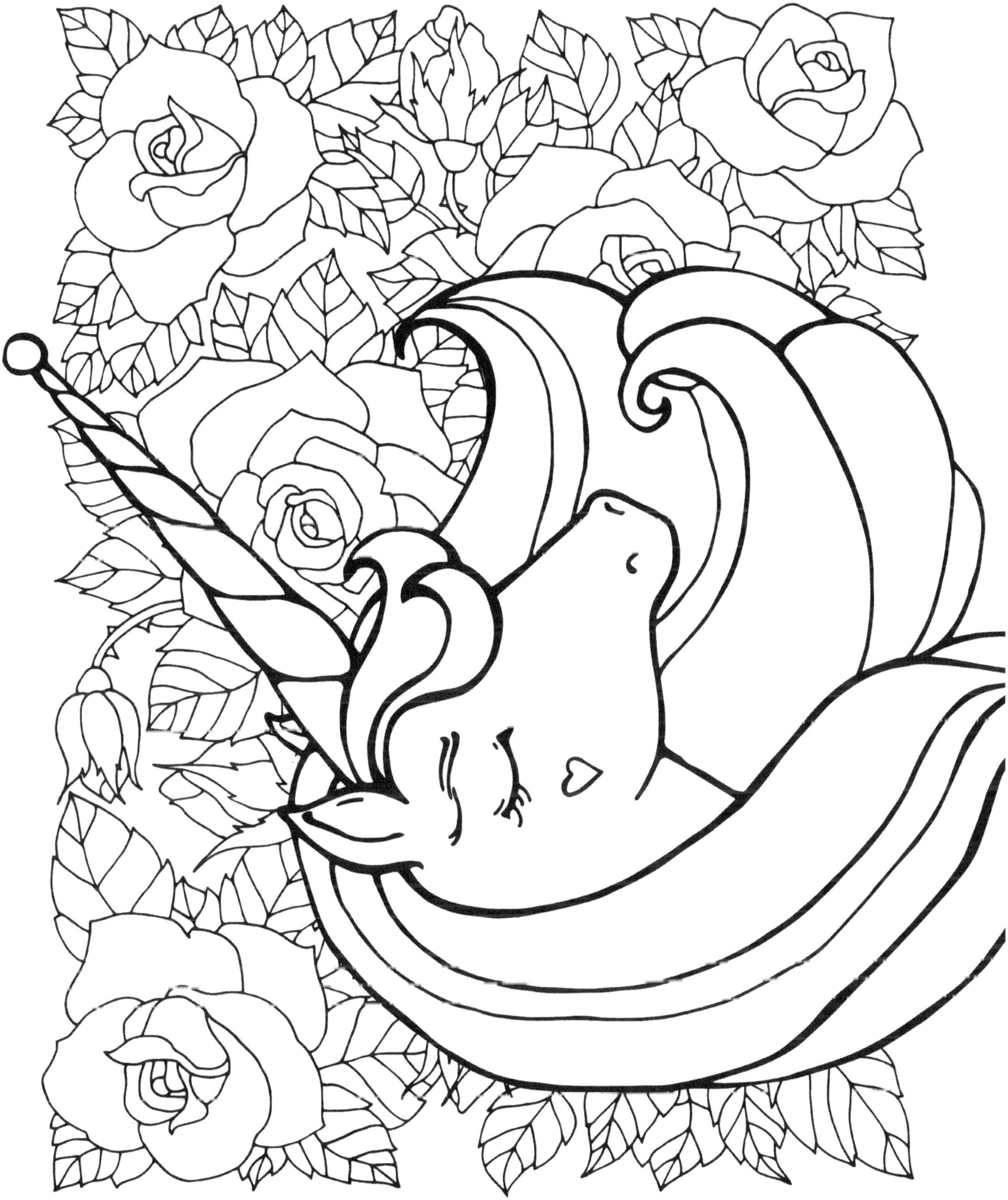

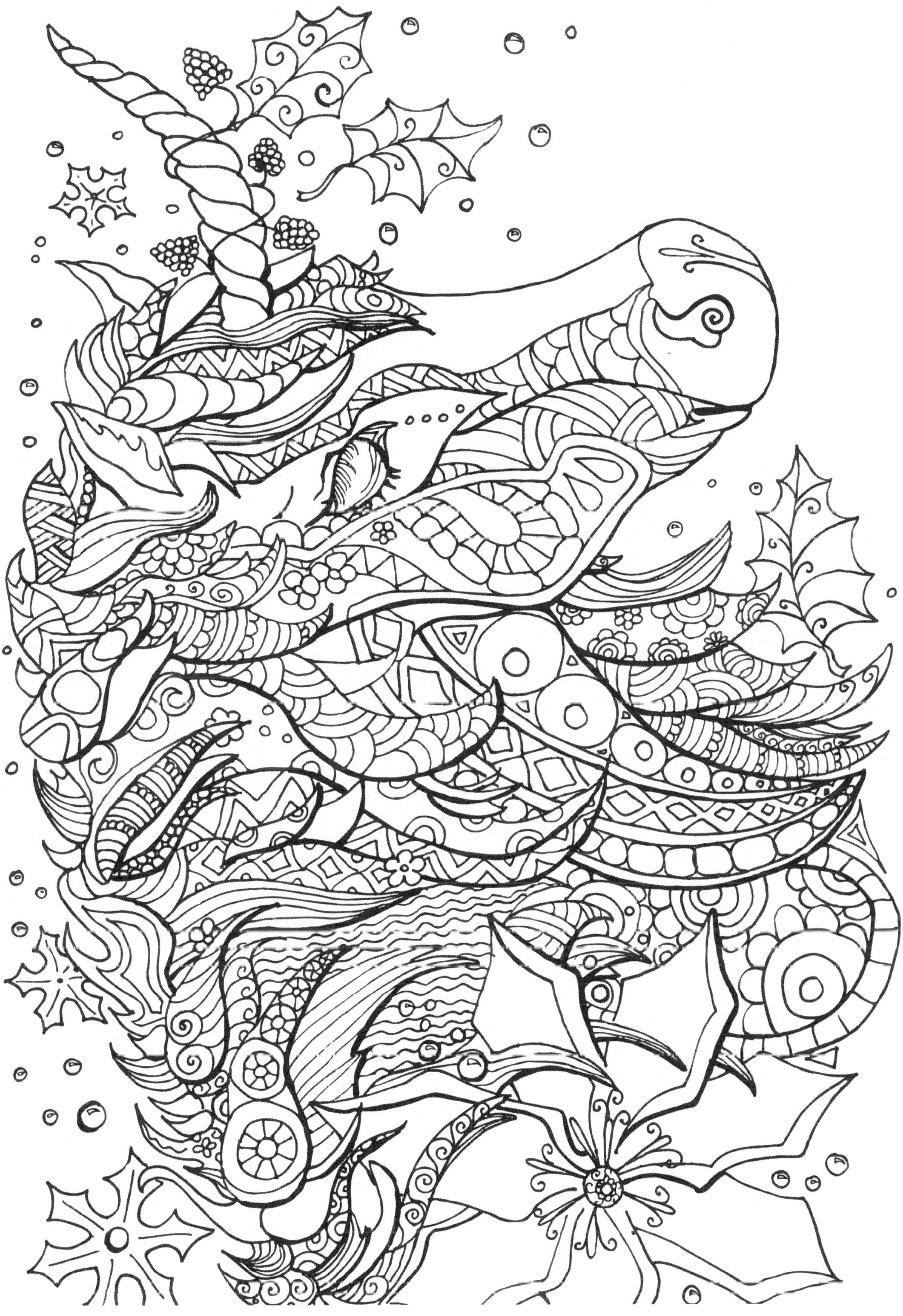

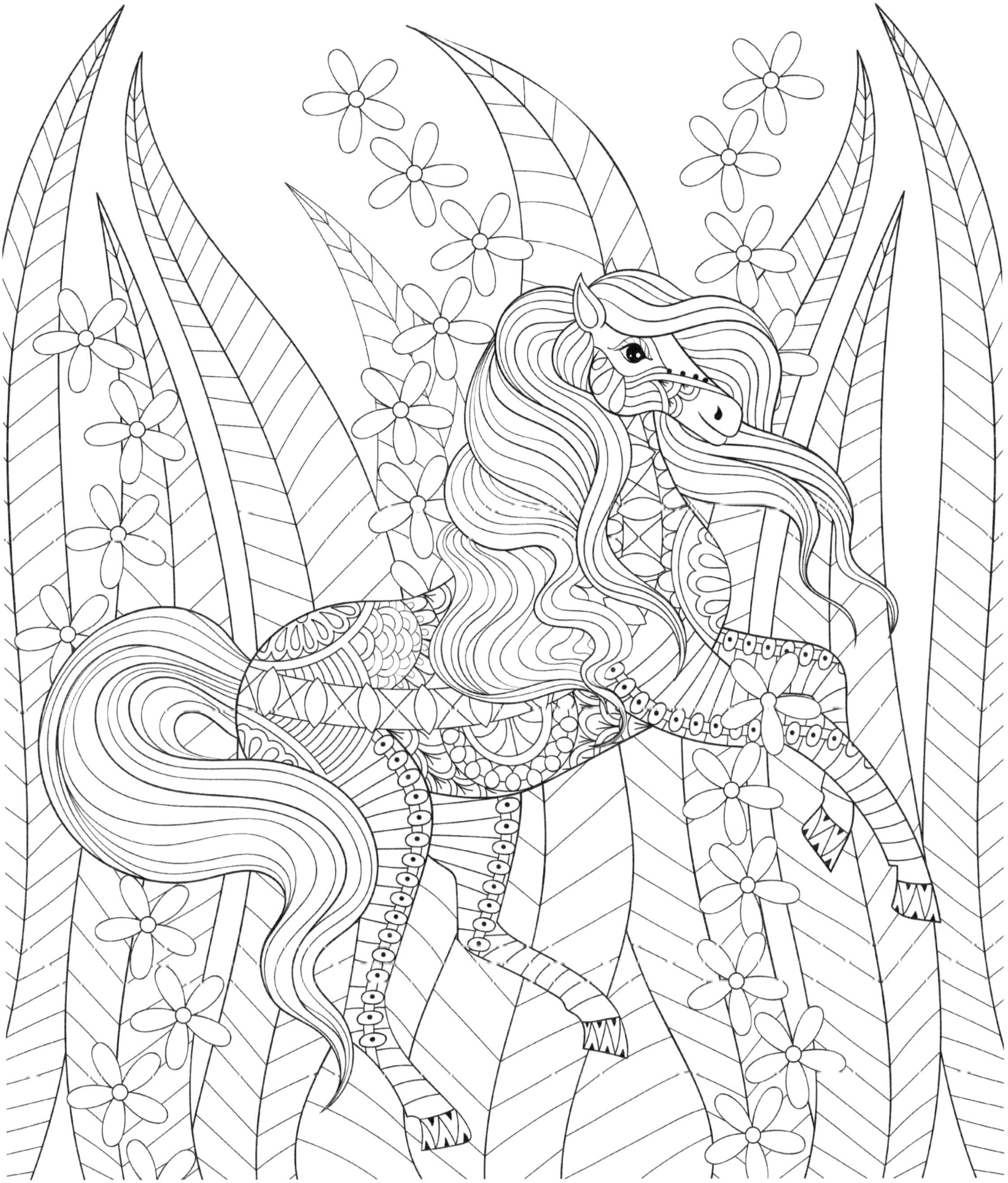

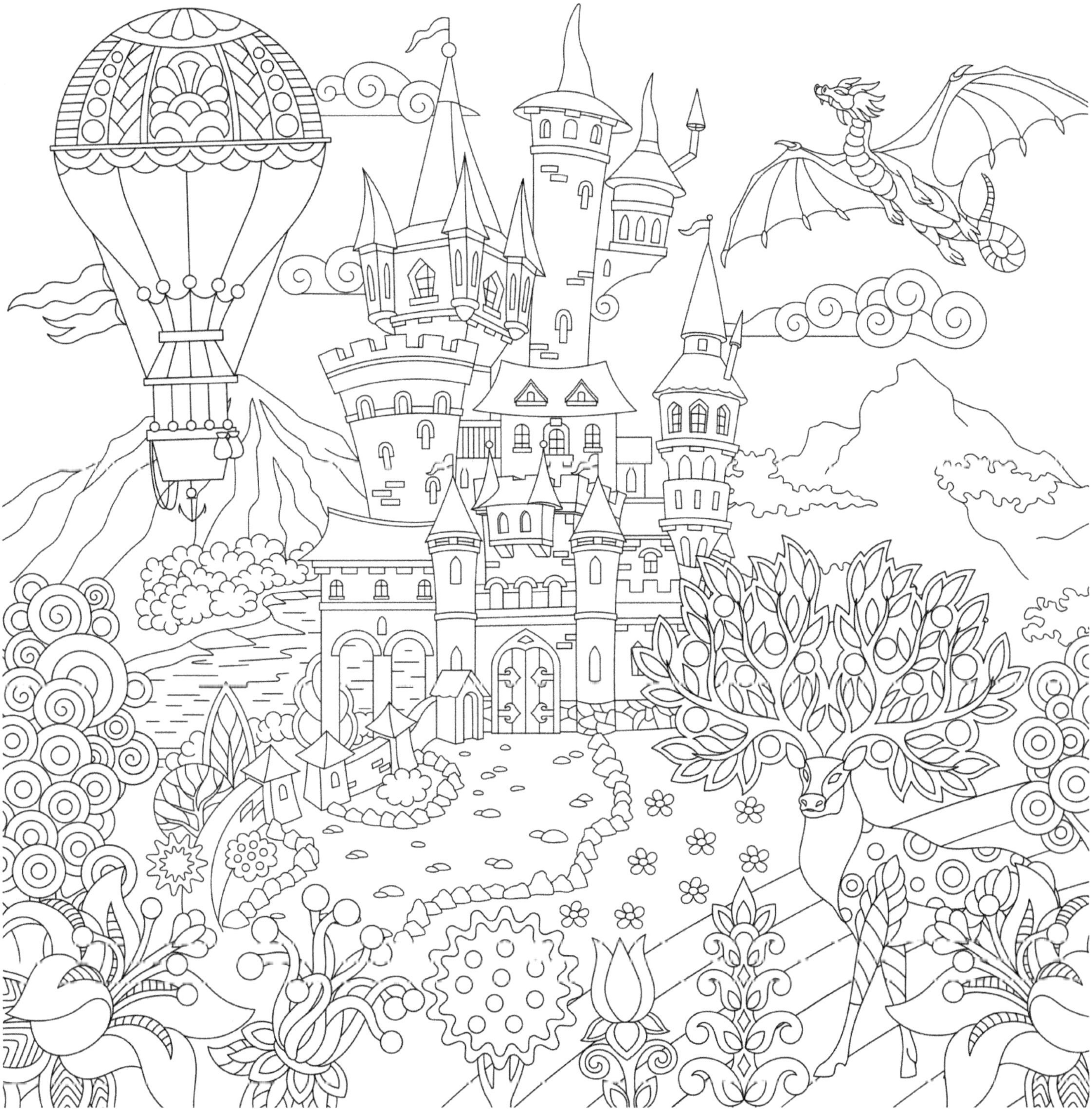

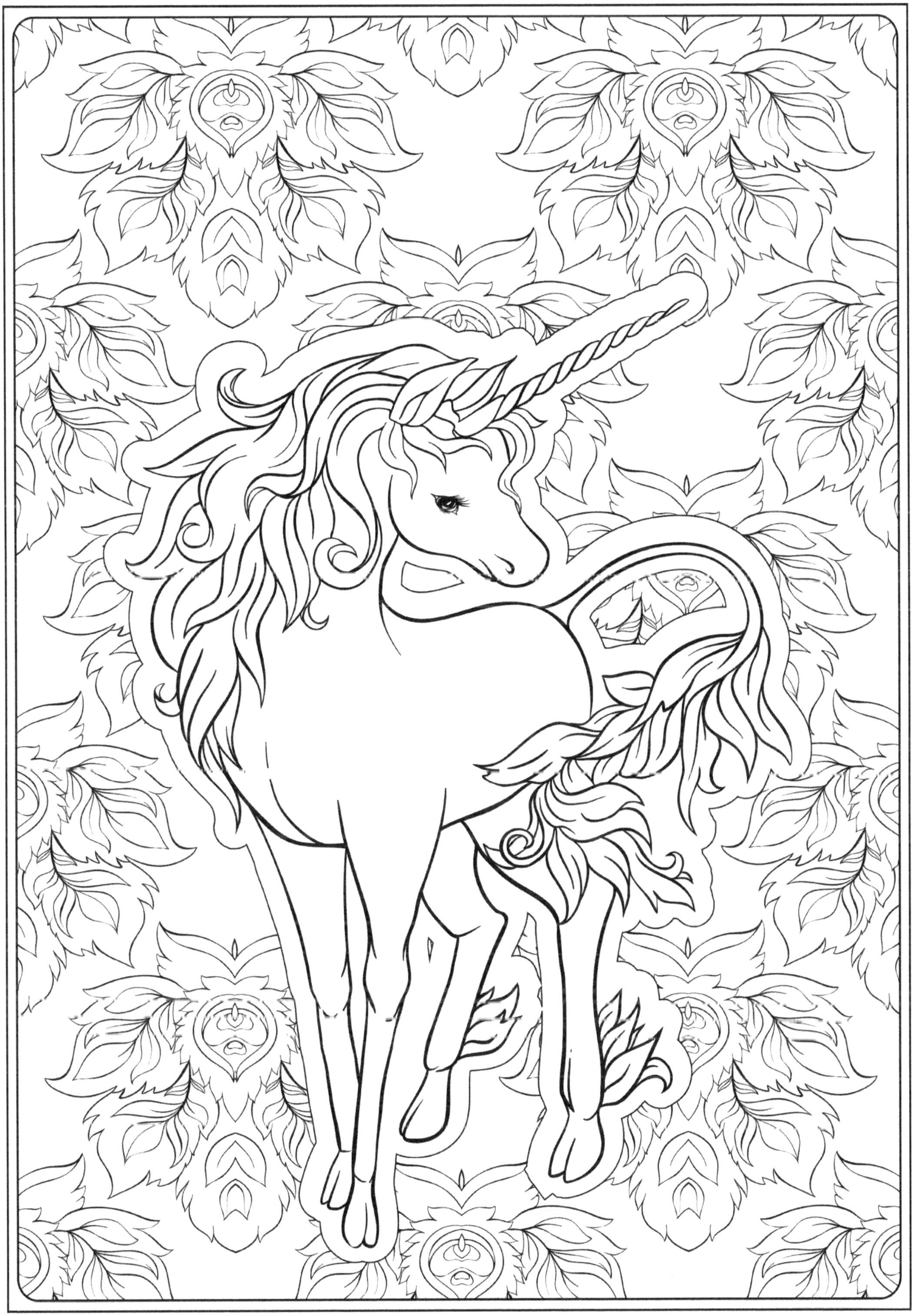

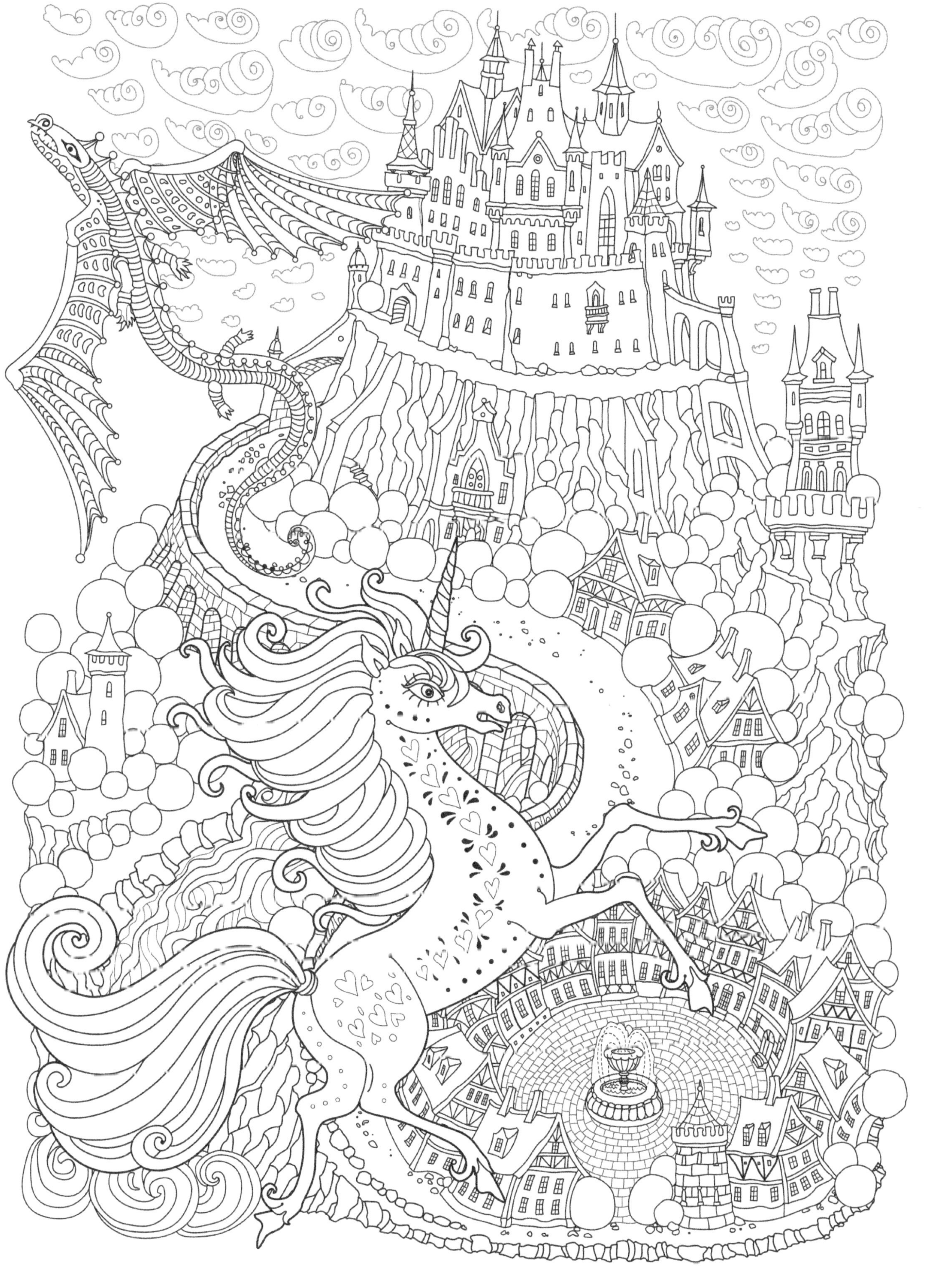

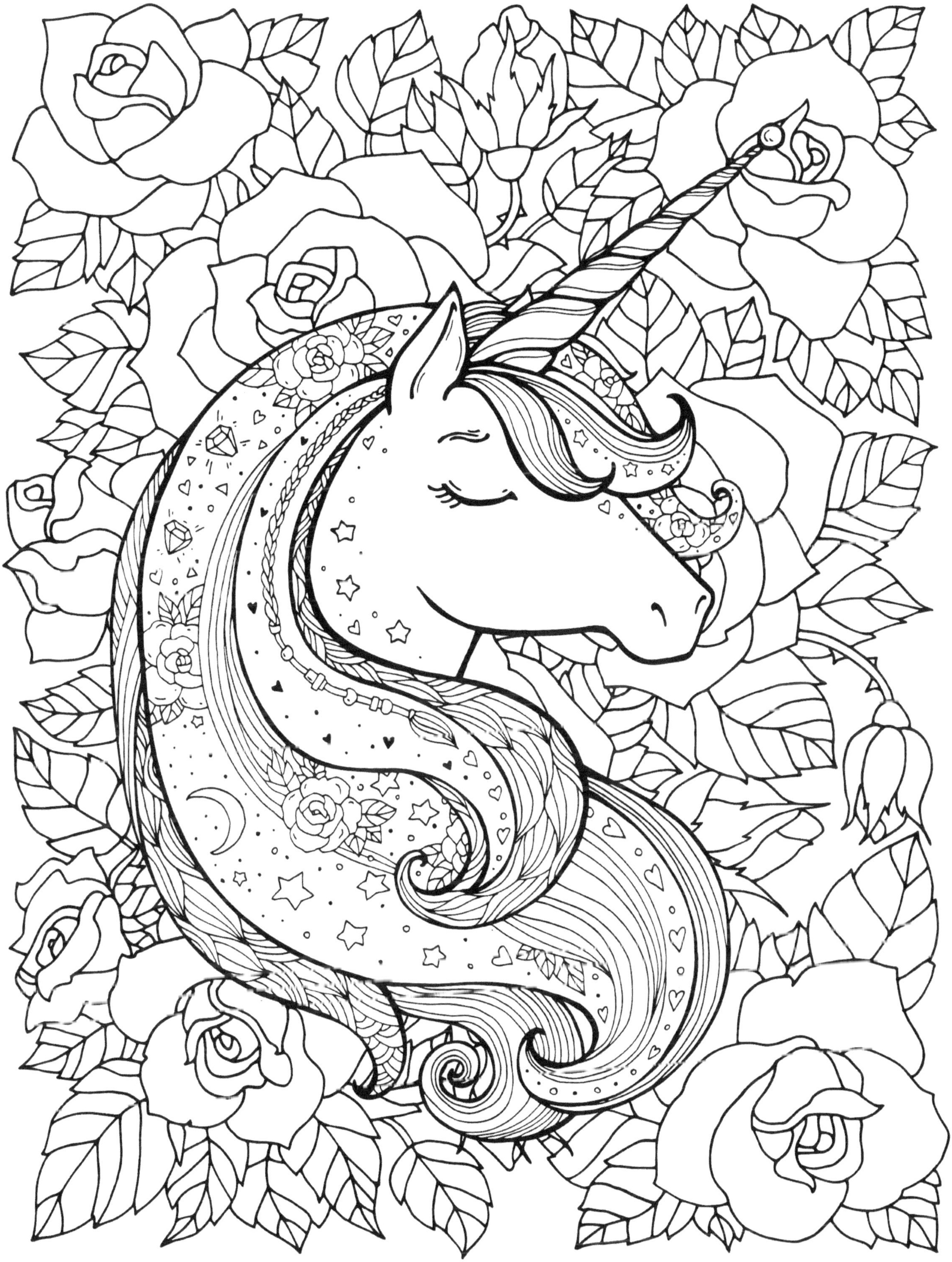

www.ingramcontent.com/pod-product-compliance
Lightning Source LLC
Chambersburg PA
CBHW080920170526
45158CB00008B/2179
* 9 7 8 1 0 7 2 3 6 3 6 0 6 *